COCKNEY KID
&
COUNTRYMEN

The Second World War
remembered by the children of
Woburn Sands and Aspley Guise

Ted Enever

The
Book
Castle

For my children, Mark and Rachel,
and to the memory of my parents.

Also by Ted Enever:
Britain's Best Kept Secret - Ultra's base at Bletchley Park.

First published March 2001 by
The Book Castle
12 Church Street
Dunstable
Bedfordshire LU5 4RU

ISBN 1 871199 89 1

Typeset & Designed by Priory Graphics
Printed by Antony Rowe Ltd.,
Chippenham, Wiltshire

ACKNOWLEDGEMENTS

When I asked via the columns of the Milton Keynes Citizen newspaper for wartime friends and classmates to assist me in the compilation of this book, I was both surprised and gratified by the response. The telephone just didn't stop ringing. To all of those with whom I had contact, may I once more say thank you and extend those thanks to others who, though not well known to me as a boy, were able to assist me greatly in my research. Within both these groups I owe special debts of gratitude to the following:

Keith Artingstall, Sam Beasley, Billy Blowes, Jim Broadbent, Bob Brown, Maurice Circuitt, Sylvia Cox, Malcolm Deacon, Denis Gurner, June Horne, Betty Hulance, Frances Jones, Lady Patricia King, Priscilla Knight, Mary Manning, George Norman, Bob and Les Page, Guin Parker, Chris Randall, Josie Rowe, Tony Walters and Mary Yates.

Many of the above were also kind enough to loan personal photographs and illustrative materials, some of which are reproduced within the text, and I am also grateful in this respect to the Woburn Sands Society and to the Milton Keynes Citizen, where my friend of long professional standing, news editor Steve Larner, was most helpful. Ruth Gill, of the Records Office of Bedfordshire County Council, gave me answers to queries very quickly, so my thanks to her, and for permission to reproduce photographs of the London Blitz, these are extended to Sarah Harding, of the Archives and Local Studies Department of the London Borough of Newham, and to Janice Mullin, of the Imperial War Museum.

To each and everyone mentioned above, to Paul Bowes and Sally Siddons of The Book Castle and to all those who have expressed an interest in this publication, may I record that this particular millennium project could not have been achieved without their help.

About the author....

Ted Enever was educated at Bedford Modern School and entered journalism in 1951 with the Bletchley District Gazette. After his two years National Service in the army he continued his career as a freelance, combining this with work in the family greengrocery business. He returned to staff journalism in 1964. In 1967 he became editor of the Bucks Standard at Newport Pagnell before joining Marshall Cavendish, the London based international publishers, as deputy managing editor. In 1971 Mr Enever joined the Inner London Education Authority as managing editor and publications which he launched and controlled won many national trade awards. In 1987 he was appointed Director of Public Affairs with the British Dental Association before joining Milton Keynes Development Corporation, two years later, where he managed all media relations and was involved in a wide range of marketing, ceremonial and public relations activities.

Retiring when the Corporation was wound up in 1992, Ted Enever was a founder member of the Bletchley Park Trust and served as its chief executive and a Trustee in its formative years. He still plays an active part in the Trust's fund raising activities and is author of a successful book detailing the setting up of the wartime code-breaking centre, 'Britain's Best Kept Secret - Ultra's Base at Bletchley Park.' He was recently made a patron of the Bletchley Park Trust.

A keen gardener and sportsman, Ted Enever is a past president of Bletchley St Martin's Bowls Club and was recently invited to become a member of the Dennyside Bowling Association, an organisation devoted to raising money for local charities with special matches throughout the country and which is limited to only 125 members nation-wide. Ted Enever is married with two children and the family lived in Bow Brickhill for many years before moving to Bletchley in 1985.

CONTENTS

INTRODUCTION

What is detailed on the following pages is not a blow by blow account or a chronicle of the events of the Second World War. It was never meant to be, for greater talent than mine has already accomplished that task, and I have taken the liberty of assuming that the reader already has some background knowledge of the causes of the conflict and of its first phase, known as the phoney war. What I hope to achieve, however, in this my personal millennium project and as we look back to the recent sixtieth anniversary of the Battle of Britain, is to give the reader a snapshot of village life in the two communities of Woburn Sands, in North Buckinghamshire, and its neighbouring village, Aspley Guise, in Bedfordshire, during the war years. More importantly, it is life as seen and remembered by those of us who were then children aged between six and perhaps twelve or thirteen, with additional material gleaned from those who were already adults and engaged in what were known as Home Front activities.

The Second World War was unique in many respects, but not least in that for the first time ordinary citizens in all walks of life found themselves caught up in the fray. No longer was it a question of two opposing armies facing each other, blasting each other to bits and the one with most men left standing the victor. Modern weaponry and the emerging technologies of the day extended the conflict away from the pitched battlefield and into civilian life. It brought the phrase 'total war' into everyday language.

Not that the two villages concerned saw horrendous enemy onslaughts or stubborn military defence by their inhabitants. But they did see a pulling together by the community in a variety of ways to assist the war effort, a trait common throughout other villages, towns and cities in the United Kingdom at that time. It coined another phrase: community spirit, achieved whilst what semblance of ordinary life could be carried on.

It is that semblance of life that I hope to communicate in the following pages as I and my parents, Londoners escaping from the Blitz, discovered the rural idyll.

Ted Enever - Bletchley, Remembrance Day, 11 November 2000

CHAPTER 1

BLITZED

At around midday on Sunday, 8 September 1940, I stood for the very first time on the Bedford-Cambridge platform of Woburn Sands station. I was tired, hungry and unsure of exactly where I was, but I knew at least that I was somewhere in Buckinghamshire, I was safe and I was with my Mum and Dad. I was six years old and only that morning we had left behind the German Blitz of London's East End.

My parents, Ted and Dolly Enever, were London Cockneys

Woburn Sands station. The building is considered to be an outstanding example of Victorian station architecture, but has played no part in the daily round of railway work for many years. What character the station complex retained has been reduced by the installation of modern platform shelters though the Station House was refurbished during 2000 and is now used as a local business centre.

1

and proud of it. Both were born within the sound of Bow bells and east of Aldgate pump, as was I, their only child, on 17 August 1934. I first saw the light of day - or more correctly, early evening - at 5.30pm at the East End Maternity Hospital in Stepney. It was the nearest maternity unit to where we lived, an East End district called Canning Town.

Canning Town sits on the northern bank of the Thames on the seaward side of the big loop in the river that creates the Isle of Dogs. It grew rapidly as an urban community in the early and mid nineteenth century as the industrial revolution of the Victorian era took hold. Shipbuilding became a profitable industry and the origins of West Ham United, the current major East End football league side, sprang from the Thames Ironworks, one such company. Even today diehard West Ham fans refer to their side as 'the Irons.'

Shipbuilding gradually gave way to the provision of deep water docks and by the early twentieth century the Royal Victoria, Royal Albert and then King George V docks became the major employers in the area.

Not that my father was a docker. He was a market trader, specialising all the year round in salad commodities - tomatoes, lettuce, cucumbers, salad onions and the like - and he and my mother made a comfortable living from their stall in Canning Town's premier market place, Rathbone Street. Backing up the stall were corner shop greengrocery premises which my grandfather and grandmother Enever ran between them in nearby Peter Street. So my heritage at a very early age seemed destined to follow in the costermonger footsteps of the Enever side of the family, though my mother's father, Sam Ager, who was a widower but then married again, was a stevedore in the docks.

There are occasions in everyone's life which, as the years advance, you can look back and recognise as defining moments or periods of time. That weekend of the 7-8 September 1940 was one such occasion for me.

September had begun in the same way as August had ended, with the Battle of Britain at its height but London seeing no mass attacks by German bombers as had been forecast and feared. Their targets, it became clear, were our fighter stations, particularly in the south-east and on the outskirts of the capital. On 23 August, however, a German bomber attacking the fighter airfields had dumped its bombs on London just to lighten its load and get away quickly from the harassing Spitfires and Hurricanes of the RAF. Prime Minister Winston Churchill promptly ordered raids on the German capital, Berlin. In retaliation, the Germans changed their tactics and London and other British cities became the prime targets. Saturday 7 September saw the first massed raids on London.

At about seven o'clock on the morning before, Friday, 6 September, the day began normally enough at the large top floor flat where we lived at number 26 in Chandler Avenue, a small avenue just off the Beckton Road, in Canning Town. My Dad was up early to go to Covent Garden market to buy his weekend supplies, leaving some part-time help he employed to get the stall from the yard behind the shop in Peter Street and set up in Rathbone Street.

My mother used Friday mornings as one of her times to do the housework and my particular treat, before school, was to be still tucked up in bed with a Mickey Mouse comic to read while she busied herself in the flat. Then it was up, breakfast, off to Beckton Road school just round the corner, then Mum went

My mother and father at the Rathbone Street stall. This photograph was taken at 8am on Good Friday 1933, when they were already engaged to be married. The wedding took place a few weeks later on Sunday 23rd May. The prices of items for sale are in pre-decimal coinage, or 'old' money as it is now called, decimal currency having been introduced in the early 1970s.

off to join Dad on the stall. At the end of the school day one of Dad's helpers would collect me from school and take me off to the stall in Rathbone Street where, with the aid of empty salad crates and other bits and pieces, I would build a den under the stall where I and my mates could hide away from the gaze of adults.

We had been at war with Germany for a year and even though I and my friends were very young children, we knew of the fall of France, of the Dunkirk evacuation and that talk of invasion was in the air. We knew that was why German bombers were pounding the fighter bases and our heroes were the Spitfire and Hurricane pilots of the day. When we were not huddled in the den under the stall we would be chasing up and

4

down the crowded pavements, arms outstretched either side, pretending we were RAF pilots in our planes shooting down the enemy bombers.

Some of us children had witnessed the real combat. Two or three weeks earlier, when the fruit picking season in Kent was underway, some of us had gone with friends and relatives to the orchards and hopfields for the traditional Cockney paid holiday of bringing in those harvests. I had gone with my Gran Enever and Mum had come down at a weekend. While she was there, and we were all in an orchard, Mum helping Gran do some picking, air raid wardens appeared blowing whistles and telling us to take cover.

The only place to go was to crawl under the trees and within a couple of minutes we could see vapour trails high in the sky and hear faint bursts of machine gun fire, sounding for all the world like a stick being rattled along a picket fence, but a long way away. Then suddenly there was the roar of an engine very low overhead.

Lying on my side just under the tree I looked up and saw a yellow-nosed German Messershmidt 109 fighter coming down in a shallow dive and trailing lots of oily smoke. As it went out of sight to crash about a mile away, its chasing Spitfire whipped over the top of our heads. Everyone cheered as we realised what had happened, it all went quiet and within a few minutes we were given the 'all clear' from the wardens and it was back to work.

By about five o'clock on that particular Friday, though, all that was in the past as the stall was packed away ready for next morning, Saturday 7 September. It was the day that the East End was to remember as Black Saturday.

For me it began as did any other Saturday. Mum needed to be at the stall early for the busiest day of the trading week so I would go with her. Sometimes, if I felt like it and my parents gave me the go-ahead, I would stand with a lettuce or something clutched in my hands, calling at passers by and willing them to buy, mimicking the actions of a stall holder. But by ten o'clock a gang of my pals would meet up with me at the stall and off we would go to Saturday morning pictures at one of the several cinemas in Canning Town. After pictures we would descend on the pie and mash shop in Rathbone Street and when a plateful of that fortifying Cockney food was inside us, we would play street games or go to one of the local parks. By late afternoon we then went our separate ways, me invariably back to the stall or to the Peter Street shop where, reunited with my parents, the working week came to an end and we went home to Chandler Avenue for a family meal.

For me, that Saturday seemed no different to any other. Mum started to cook the meal, Dad counted up the week's takings, and I helped by stacking the silver and copper into pounds or shilling units. I didn't realise at the time but it was a marvellous way of getting to grips with basic arithmetic.

By now it was a little after five o'clock and the sirens began to wail their warning. We didn't take a lot of notice. Warnings had come and gone like this since the war started but London had not been attacked. Everyone was nervous of a bombing attack, of course, and we had taken to our Anderson shelter in the back yard many times. But when no raids materialised early in the war, the general consensus was that you carried on as normal. So Mum carried on cooking, I was playing with some toy cowboys and indians and a model stagecoach, but Dad said he thought he could hear aircraft engines.

Aircraft over London at that time were by now recognised as our own, other than for the single bomber that dumped its bombs on 23 August. However, that nervousness of bombing was nevertheless there, particularly having learned from newsreels at the cinema of the fate of places like Rotterdam and Warsaw, bombed to rubble by Germany's Luftwaffe aircraft.

Dad decided he would go downstairs to listen at the front door which opened directly onto the street. Mum and I stayed in the kitchen. A couple of minutes later Dad came back to say he thought he could hear explosions on the south side of the river, over Woolwich way, and perhaps we ought to go into the Anderson shelter just to be on the safe side. The Anderson was made of a series of curved corrugated iron sheets bolted to straight sided sheets which were buried in the ground over a dug out pit. In fact, many people referred to their Anderson as

Job done. A German Heinkel 111 bomber turns and makes its way over the Isle of Dogs and Limehouse Reach in September 1940 after its attack. The Royal group of docks, close to where we lived, is just out of the picture, middle right.

the dug-out. It was to prove a very effective bomb shelter for thousands of families. The problem was, not everybody had them, either through lack of outdoor space or because they made other arrangements for nightly shelter.

I gathered up my toys and Mum went into the bedroom to get some blankets and pillows should we need to bed down, though in truth I think my parents expected the 'all clear' to sound quite quickly, as it usually did. As we busied ourselves

Dad went down again to the front door. Then suddenly he screamed up the stairs: 'Dolly, get down, down; quick, quick!' Mum rushed out of the bedroom, scooped me up in her arms in the kitchen, and carried me to the landing at the top of the stairs. Then, it seemed, all hell broke loose.

My father had moved away from the open front door to turn and run to the foot of the stairs, but the open door did him no favours. The first of the bombs fell on a house almost opposite and it virtually disappeared. The blast, coming through the open front door to the flat, blew Dad along the passageway and threw him with sickening force against the heavy bannister post. A smoker who rolled his own cigarettes, he carried his tobacco and cigarette papers in a silver box kept in his waistcoat pocket. He still had his waistcoat on at the time and the tobacco box took the force of the impact and was promptly flattened. It was never any use after that but it stopped his ribs from being crushed and probably saved his life.

As he picked himself up he was amazed to find both mother and me alongside him in a heap on the passage floor. The return suction of the blast had whisked us both feet first down the stairs into the passage, but we were unhurt. The return suction had also banged the front door shut but we could see the flames of burning houses nearby through the door's shattered glass panels.

The elderly couple who were the downstairs occupants of the house were lucky to be visiting relatives that weekend. Our normal way of getting to the back yard was via our own set of outdoor steps leading from the rear of the flat but the quickest way out now was to use our fellow tenants' ground floor side door.

We crawled along the passageway to the door as the crump of bombs seemed to come from everywhere, the noise getting louder by the minute. Broken glass from the front door panels littered the passage floor and we had to move carefully not to get cut. As we crawled toward the door we were showered in plaster from where the ceilings had shattered. But apparently I merely asked, in all innocence: 'Are we playing Indians?'

We got to the door which had become jammed by the blast and Dad had to splinter the lock with a small axe taken from the coal-hole under the stairs. As he forced the door open and we made a dash for the Anderson it looked as if the whole world was

The first bombs of Black Saturday, 7th September 1940, come down on London's docks as merchant ships are moored at their berths.

on fire. Buildings everywhere seemed to be ablaze and the sky was red and orange from the glare of the fires wherever you looked. We made it to the shelter and spent the next twelve hours wondering if we would come out alive. Lying on a bunk in the shelter I vividly remember seeing the side lift up from the blast of bombs falling nearby and, just inches from my nose, little trickles of earth and sand fall on to my blanket before the side settled back in place. The raid just went on and on as the German bombers came over in waves.

Germany had changed its bombing tactics. London and its

commercial installations, such as the East End docks, were to be main targets.

The pall of smoke hanging over the East End and its docks in the early evening of Black Saturday is framed by the Tower of London and Tower Bridge. A Fire Brigade officer sent out the message: 'Send every pump you've got. The whole world's on fire!'

The docks, warehouses, offices, gasworks and electricity stations serving the East End were ravaged that night, as well as thousands of ordinary homes. The gas main running down the middle of the Beckton Road, only about seventy yards from where we were, had caught a direct hit and escaping gas had ignited and set off other endless fires. The warehouses on both sides of the river were some of the worst conflagrations as sugar, timber, rope, textiles, alcohol and all manner of other goods caught alight. Flames shot hundreds of feet in the air and hurled burning debris and embers which started yet more fires. Thousand of rats, driven from their riverside nests by the flames, were everywhere, both in the water and the dockside streets.

The carnage and damage caused that night by both high

11

explosive and incendiary bombs was appalling. By the early hours of the next morning some 430 East Londoners were dead and another 1600 injured. Many thousands more had lost their homes. Black Saturday had earned its name.

At 5.30am on the Sunday morning, after the bombing had stopped, we crawled out of the Anderson. The roof of the house had gone, all the windows were smashed, there was debris everywhere and I remember I could see nearby streets quite clearly because there were no houses in the way now to block the view. They had just disappeared overnight.

We inched our way up the broken stairs of what had been our home, picking our way through the rubble and debris of what were tidy rooms only the evening before. My parents packed a few belongings as best they could before Dad then dashed off to see if my two sets of grandparents were alright and to let them know that he was getting Mum and me out of London that very day. We were going, he told them, to a place called Woburn Sands in Buckinghamshire, where one of his Covent Garden friends enjoyed weekends away. 'It's about forty miles,' he told them. 'Far away enough to be safe, near enough to be able to get back here as and when.' He urged them to come with us but both declined, as did his elder brother Jim who lived with his wife and two children only a half-a-mile away in Hermit Road. The homes of both my grandparents and Uncle Jim had luckily escaped virtually undamaged.

We trekked from the flat the long way round to Barking Road. The normal, short way was still blocked by the flames from the broken gas main in Beckton Road. Fire engines, ambulances and civil defence crews seemed everywhere and dead bodies and injured people were being brought out from

The life-saving Anderson shelter. These two women emerge unscathed from their 'dug-out' whilst around them everything is reduced to rubble.

A typical East End scene after the Black Saturday raids. What few possessions can be saved are piled in the middle of the street should weakened masonry suddenly collapse and cause more damage. The grim reality of war is etched on the faces of both residents and wardens.

the ruins of collapsed and damaged buildings. I was so tired I could have gone to sleep amongst the rubble.

The roads were in chaos and there were many people like us who, having lost their homes, were looking to get away from the area for safety. Epping Forest seemed a favourite destination. There were no buses running so Dad flagged down a hurrying taxi cab whose driver only stopped because he literally barred his path. The driver said he wasn't taking any fares; well, not until Dad asked him to name his own price. It

Damage to Canning Town homes in Victoria Dock Road caused by the first wave of bombers.

cost my father ten pounds that morning to get us from Canning Town to Euston station. That was the equivalent then of about five or six weeks wages and about twenty times the normal going rate. But you couldn't really blame the driver, given the circumstances.

Fire hoses snaked across the roads all the way through an East End unrecognisable from the day before. Some parts of our route were totally blocked by the rubble of demolished and damaged buildings so we had to make detours, but once into the City of London the damage was a lot less. It was clear

Youngsters gather to inspect damage to Mortlake Road, Canning Town, on the morning of Saturday 8th September. Bomb blast often had a peculiar effect of taking out buildings completely and leaving others virtually untouched, as are the adjacent premises carrying the advertising signs.

that the East End docks and Surrey docks, and the commercial facilities associated with them, had borne the brunt of the damage inflicted by the waves of German bombers that had appeared over the capital.

The 7 September raid marked the beginning of more than sixty successive nights of bombing which were to engulf all areas of London. The City of London district around St Paul's, the west end, south and north London and even the suburbs all became targets. Buckingham Palace was bombed within a week of that first attack and moved the Queen, now the Queen

16

Mother, to comment: 'Now I can look the East End in the face.'

We finally made it to Euston and caught the train to Bletchley. I slept as far as Watford but then woke up to a panorama of green fields, hedges and trees under a clear blue sky and bright sunshine. The train chuffed its way through Hertfordshire, past the then Ovaltine egg farm at Kings Langley and the old castle ruins at Berkhamsted, then went through the Tring and Leighton Buzzard tunnels before reaching Bletchley.

At Bletchley we changed trains, crossing the wooden footbridge from the London platforms to find platform 7 where the Oxford-Cambridge branch line would take us to Woburn Sands. My sleep on the train from Euston had perked me up a bit and though I was still tired I was eager to see the sea. Well, a place called Woburn Sands was at the seaside, wasn't it? We travelled through Fenny Stratford where I spotted both canal and river, but no, that wasn't the sea, then went swiftly past the wooden sleepers by the track which I was to learn later was the halt at Bow Brickhill. But still the only water in view as we pulled in to Woburn Sands station was the flooded clay pit of a disused brick works. The works chimneys, now long since demolished, were still standing then, and poor mother thought she was merely exchanging one urban Luftwaffe target for another!

She changed her mind, though, when the peace and quiet of a village Sunday morning became evident as the train pulled away to leave us standing on the platform. There were few other passengers for Woburn Sands and there were no name signs up at the station; like road signs they had all been taken down as the war progressed in an attempt to confuse the enemy should we be invaded. But we knew we had arrived by

17

the sing-song voice of the train guard telling us we were at 'Wobbly Sands' - or so it seemed to my young ears.

The signalman came down from his box to reopen the crossing gates to traffic - of which there was little, being a Sunday - and we moved towards the nearby Station Hotel. Here my parents enquired about the possibility of booking a room but were told by the publican, Fred Hinde, that there were no vacancies. He advised trying the next pub in the village, The Weathercock. We had no luck here either, but were directed just across the road to Cherry Tree cottage, the home of a Mrs Medcalf and next door to a dairy-cum-tea rooms owned by a local farmer, Mr Fred Baker. Mrs Medcalf was our saviour. For the next three nights she somehow made room for us while Dad sorted us out.

While Mum and I rested with Mrs Medcalf on the Sunday afternoon, Dad went across to The Weathercock for a well-earned pint. Following what he had gone through, the first pint led to one or two more and he was not used to the strength of country beer. At closing time he wandered back toward the station and had a deep, relaxing sleep stretched out on the grass of the Woburn Sands Recreation Ground.

When he woke up it was nearly five o'clock, a full day since our horror of the bombing began. It was then he discovered that his wallet, containing close on £300, was missing. Like many people of the time he held no bank account. Money was earned, money was spent, and what you saved you kept tucked away somewhere at home. The £300, a tidy sum in those days, was his business stock money and savings. In a blind panic, he rushed back to The Weathercock.

CHAPTER 2

CONKERS AND FROG SPAWN

The Weathercock was, of course, closed when he reached the bar door. There was no all-day opening then, pub hours were very regulated and it would be two hours before Mr Edward (Teddy) Martin, the then landlord, would pull the bolts on the front door.

Father made his way round to the back, up the little alleyway space that divided the pub from Les Blanshard's garage next door. He remembered taking his wallet from his pocket to pay for beer, so he surmised it must have gone missing in the

The Weathercock pub at Woburn Sands today. In 1940 there were no baskets of flowers on the forecourt, the open space in front of the building looked upon as part of the road.

pub. What he didn't know was had he just lost it or had someone stolen it by picking his pocket? Thankfully, he was soon put out of his agony. He banged on the back door of the pub and it was Mr Martin himself who opened it. Before Dad could say a word, Mr Martin said: 'Is this what you're looking for, son?' He produced the wallet and as father stammered his thanks and began to check the contents he was told: 'It's all there, chum. You left it on the corner of the bar. I hope you soon get sorted out. Now go and get some more rest, you look as if you need it!'

Mrs Medcalf's Cherry Tree cottage. The cherry tree in the front garden has long since gone and the neighbouring properties are now a fish and chip shop and a carpet store.

After the three nights of sleeping on the floor of Mrs Medcalf's cottage, rooms were made available to us almost opposite, at 62 Station Road, by Alec and Rene Circuitt. It was to be the start of a large chunk of the Enever family turning its back on the East End and embracing a whole new way of life in the country.

The former home of the Circuitt family, 62 Station Road, Woburn Sands. Now a ladies boutique, in 1940 the front of the property featured a boarded up area stretching up to the pavement, for it was once a shop which was rammed by a passing lorry. This area was used as a garage and for general storage by Mr Circuitt. The Enever families lived upstairs on the left.

Alec and Rene were about the same age as my parents and had children of their own, so I had built in mates almost from day one. The eldest was Maurice, a few months older than me, then Brian, a couple of years younger. Iris came next, followed by Michael, who was then just a toddler. Later their family was to see further additions with the births of Gerald, Grace and Kenneth. All the boys were destined to grow up to be competent local footballers, though sadly Gerald developed heart problems and died while still a young man.

Maurice lost no time in hiking me out to meet the neighbouring kids, the eldest, and the one we all looked up to being Francis Nursall, who with his two sisters, Vera and Ruby, lived in a cottage in the little cul-de-sac called West Road, just around the corner. Francis, being that bit older, had a good grasp of what was happening in the war and was very patriotic. One of his favourite games was to get Maurice, Brian

21

and me - and sometimes an even younger ginger-haired lad called Les Butcher whose family also lived in West Road - into a parade line of make believe soldiers. He would have us march up and down West Road singing at the tops of our voices all sorts of wartime songs, including the words to the music of the National Savings campaign: 'Saving, saving, helping to win the war; whenever you think you've saved enough, go on and save some more!'

Woburn Sands Square as it looked more than sixty years ago before the War Memorial was moved to its present home close to Shelton Court.

Woburn Sands takes its name from neighbouring Woburn, an old market town, and the greensand ridge of woodland, mostly the property of the Duke of Bedford's estates, to the south. Originally known as Hog Sty End because of the number of pigs kept locally, it was an area or 'end' of Wavendon, the next village north. It prospered to become a village in its own right with the coming of the railway in the 19th century and its centre, as with its neighbouring and much older village of

Aspley Guise, was The Square. The Square straddled the main Woburn to Newport Pagnell road and leading from it were roads to Bow Brickhill, Aspley Heath and Aspley Guise.

The High Street, Woburn Sands. This photograph is believed to be just post-war, given the style of vehicles and the fact that vehicle ownership at the time was obviously not so great as after the 1960's.

I found my new village life now virtually free of the traffic noises of London, though the Woburn - Newport Pagnell road, of which Station Road was a part, was a major feeder and turn-off for the Watling Street at Hockliffe and Heath and Reach, so heavy lorries did rumble along now and then. So did the occasional green double-decker bus to Aylesbury or Bedford, and seeing green buses was a novelty. London buses were red. But that constant hum of traffic noise so obvious in my native East End was no longer there. Everything seemed so quiet and peaceful. Then there was the recreation ground in which to play, only a stone's throw away; bird song and the sounds of cockerels crowing in the morning; and of great fascination, the study of the patterns made by fine grains of sand in the gutters and on the pavement, swept down by the wind and the rain from the sandhills at the top of the village. Life, it seemed, was suddenly idyllic, with only one cloud on the horizon. School!

While mother made enquiries during our first week in Woburn Sands about getting me in to the local school, Aspley Heath, my father made two trips back to Canning Town to see what could be salvaged from the damaged premises of both our home and the shop and yard in Peter Street. The answer was very little, other than one or two pieces of furniture and other personal items which had not 'disappeared' from the empty premises, for looting became commonplace. The trips were naturally made during the day, when there were no enemy aircraft overhead, for every night, without fail, the Dorniers and the Heinkels came back to bring more terror from the skies. When father tried to claim from the relevant authorities and insurers for loss of stock and war damage, he was told that salad items, fruit and vegetables were classed as perishable goods, therefore no compensation in any way was payable.

As the German bombers continued to pound the dock area, other parts of London began to suffer, too. Organised evacuation by the local council, begun in September 1939, was stepped up as more and more people lost their homes and all their possessions.

One part of the evacuation exercise in Canning Town saw several hundred mothers and children being sent to Hallsville Road school to await a fleet of coaches destined to take them to safety. Somebody along the chain of command between Council Office and coach operator got it wrong, and the coaches were directed to Camden Town, in north London, not Canning Town, in the east. The delay resulted in the mothers and children having to wait at the school overnight and they were caught up in yet another air raid. The school took a direct hit and almost everyone was killed.

By this time my Enever Grandparents and my Uncle Jim, his wife and their two small children, decided to join us at Woburn Sands, though my Mother's Father and Step-mother were

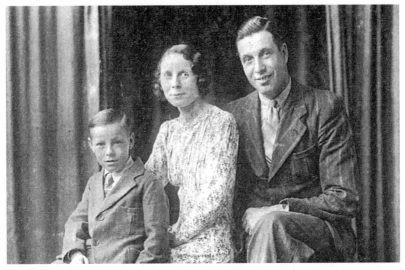

The worries of the Blitz behind us. Mother, father and a well-scrubbed youngster in 1941, just before we moved to Aspley Guise. The photograph was taken at Mr Anderson's studio in Station Road, almost opposite Dr Furber's home and surgery at Jackdaws House.

determined to stay on, at least for the time being, arguing that their Anderson shelter was safe from almost anything but a direct hit. As events were to unfold, their reasoning was right. They saw out the whole Blitz, and the later bomb and rocket attacks, from the safety of the Anderson, though they had more than one or two very near misses.

So Gran and Grandfather Enever, Uncle Jim, Aunt Vi and my two young cousins joined us at 62 Station Road, thanks again to the help of Alec and Rene Circuitt. And I joined Maurice and a host of other new friends at Aspley Heath school.

Aspley Heath School in 1935 when the children were issued with commemorative George Vth Jubilee medals. The area being used is the senior boys playground which fronted Woburn Road. The senior girls area is behind the wire fence. The sloping ground, top left, became the school garden and was put to productive use during the war years.

The headmaster was John Codd, who always seemed to us youngsters an austere man with a penchant for wearing tweed suits. But I began my country schooling with the already established six year-olds in the junior class taught by Mrs Day, the wife of Walter Day, a superb cabinet maker and carpenter who lived at Aspley Guise.

My first day at school was one of total bewilderment. My London teachings had followed the lines of what is now called nursery school. Here at Aspley Heath I was plunged straight into 'proper' education. I found I was a bit of a dunce, to say the least.

Everybody, it seemed, could read and write better than me, and in one early spelling test we were told to put a dash if we did not know the answer. I didn't even know what a 'dash' was, so for most of the answers I laboriously wrote d-a-s-h and hoped I had managed to spell the word correctly! The only area in which I held my own was

The pre-war staff at Aspley Heath School. Left to right, back: Mr Cooper, Miss Peacock, Miss Newman, Miss Wells; front: Mrs Neville, Mr Codd and an unknown lady.

simple addition and subtraction - those Saturdays helping Dad count up the stall takings were suddenly in my favour.

That late summer drifted into autumn and my father got a job driving a horse and cart around Woburn Sands and the neighbouring villages hawking bags of coal for Franklins, a Bedford-based coal merchant. Franklins were one of three coal merchants using the small sidings at Woburn Sands station, the coal being delivered in bulk in railway trucks. The other two merchants were Tompkins and Bliss, with the Franklins yard run by a gentleman named Percy Alban.

Stabling for the horse was convenient, just on the other side of the Station Hotel and right next to Mr Joe Payne's blacksmith shop which was sited at the entrance to Dudley's tile yard. I spent many happy hours with Dad at the end of his working day helping him to bed down the big bay shire horse. I helped with the feeding, grooming and the necessary mucking out and my love of horses, begun then, continues to this day.

All of the old stabling and tile yard area is currently part of the Plysu factory site.

Walking to school one morning, with the leaves on the trees gradually turning to colours I had never even dreamed of, Maurice told me: 'Conkers will be ready soon!' Again my city ignorance was apparent. 'What's conkers?' I asked.

The then home of the late Dr Brian Furber, who at the time was serving in the RAF, was Jackdaws House, on the right hand side of Station Road - 'our' side - as we walked from number 62 to school, and almost the last property before we reached Theydon Avenue. Dr Furber was a much respected GP, a tall, bespectacled man with a booming voice who was no mean cricketer, and his home and adjoining surgery lay back from the road. The front garden sported horse chestnut trees. Maurice told me in about two sentences flat the origins of the word 'conkers' and the uses made of them by small boys. It also became very clear that to get them from Dr Furber's garden meant some risk.

The front garden of Jackdaws House looking today much as it did sixty years ago. The horse chestnut trees, with conkers forming, are to the left of the picture.

It was then I learned the meaning of the word 'trespass' and the consequences of being hauled before the local magistrate at Woburn. Of course, it was all greatly exaggerated. I have no doubt that if Mrs Furber had ever spotted us in the front garden scrounging the fallen conkers, the most we would have got was a good telling off. But as I remember, we were never apparently spotted. I quickly learned the art of putting a skewer through the conker, stringing it accordingly and then doing battle with challengers all and sundry. Not that I was ever any good.

The game of conkers, as I am sure everyone knows, involves the two protagonists taking it in turns to swipe at the strung conker of the other. You let your conker dangle from its string clenched in your fist while your opponent strikes. Then you get your turn, and so it goes on until one of the conkers splits and is destroyed under the rain of blows. While my opponents landed hefty whacks with their conkers on mine, I usually seemed to miss. There were these tales of kids having a 'tenner' or a 'sixer' or whatever - conkers which had come unscathed and victorious through that number of contests - but I think the best I ever had was a 'twoer'. It was said that if you baked the conkers or doused them in vinegar it made them tougher and less liable to split, but I never tried either method myself.

There were also some good horse chestnut trees on the other side of the road, further up where the retirement home now stands and before you get to the shops in Woburn Sands High Street. But somehow that area always seemed more open to eyes than Dr Furber's garden, so we seldom set to plundering conkers from there. To this day though, when autumn comes round and the conkers litter the ground around Church Green, near my Bletchley home, I just have to pick some up and enjoy looking at their beautiful, shining, chestnut-brown colour. I collect them for my great-grandson; and I think of Dr Furber and his garden.

It was about this time, the autumn of 1940, that we were suddenly sent home from school early one day. There seemed to be some sort of panic generally and as we all spilled out of Mrs Day's classroom, into the playground and then to the Sandy Lane entrance to school, we were surprised to find parents waiting to collect us. Maurice's father, Alec, who was an air raid warden, had even brought out his car, which had been garaged since shortly after the outbreak of war. We knew then that something serious was afoot and as Maurice, Brian, myself and others piled into the car, we were told that invasion was imminent. I don't think any of us knew what 'imminent' meant, but we grasped the gist of what Mr Circuitt was telling us as he instructed us to lay on the floor of the car as he took us home. The threat of Germany invading Britain then was still very real, although we know now that Germany had by then abandoned such plans. How or why we were all suddenly and dramatically caught up in an invasion scare that day I still don't know, but it might well have been the same day that the bombs dropped on Aspley Guise, an incident recalled in more detail in Chapter 5.

Christmas came and I felt pleased with myself to be cast as one of the older shepherds in the class nativity play. I had to tell George Savage, one of my classmates playing another shepherd: 'You young ones go and follow the star. The journey is too far for me.' I must have practised those words a million times!

After what I remember as a somewhat austere Christmas,

Bedfordshire County Council

ASPLEY GUISE AND ASPLEY HEATH INVASION COMMITTEE

Important Notice to Householders

The following information is issued by the INVASION COMMITTEE for the Parishes of Aspley Guise and Aspley H ath, and is intended to prevent confusion should the district be isolated and normal supplies be cut off by enemy action of whatever nature.

You are asked to read this handbill carefully and to put it in a safe place so that it will be available for reference should the occasion arise.

If the district is threatened, our Honorary Food Organiser, Mr. F. N. Walton, O.B.E., has full authority under the Ministry of Food to take whatever action he considers necessary to control all food in the shops in the Parishes, and to ensure its fair distribution.

GROCERIES, PROVISIONS AND MEAT.

All Shops will be closed. Food will be pooled and as soon as it has been ascertained what stocks are available, supplies will be issued equally and fairly to residents : no preference will be given to registered customers.

Bullocks, sheep, pigs and fowls can be requisitioned by the Hon. Food Organiser and killed locally.

Distribution will be undertaken by the shops under police supervision.

Householders must bring their own baskets, bags, basins, tins, etc., to hold loose stuffs, as no parcel can be packed.

The notice issued to all householders in neighbouring Aspley Guise when the threat of invasion was very real. The notice ran to three pages - shown is the first - and gave precise details of how supplies of food, water and power would be administered. It also called upon all able bodied people to help with the digging of slit trenches for defence, if necessary.

31

for rationing now was really beginning to bite as our shipping experienced heavy losses to the German U-Boats, the early months of 1941 gave me some educational hope. In class we worked some subjects by being split into two groups, A and B, the A group being the more advanced. Thanks to Mrs Day's excellent teaching, my reading and writing had improved considerably and when she told me that in future I would be working with the A group permanently, I went home as proud as a peacock.

Spring came, and with it yet new adventures and things to absorb. My learned tutor, Maurice, showed me birds' nests, primroses and bluebells growing in the woods, lambs, piglets and calves in the fields and the one thing I will never, ever forget seeing for the first time. Frogs spawn!

Spring Grove is only a few steps from 62 Station Road and in those days was a cul-de-sac shaped a bit like a walkingstick. The straight end met Station Road, and there were one or two houses along the straight part, including a bungalow lived in by a delightful old gentleman named Mr Hawes who, we kids believed, was the finest fisherman in the world. We would watch in envy over his garden gate as he dried off his nets and packed his rods away after a seemingly bountiful expedition.

Where the handle of the walking stick began to take shape there was a white painted house whose front windows looked straight up Spring Grove toward Station Road. When you turned past the house the horticultural nursery of Mr White, who also owned the fruit and veg shop in the High Street, was to your right behind the hedge, and the cul-de-sac then ended abruptly in a screen of trees which partly surrounded a large pond. The pond itself, I believe, might well have been at the far end of Dr Furber's garden, or was at least in the garden of one of the adjacent houses. It was in this pond that Maurice said we would find frogs spawn.

I remember looking at him blankly, yet again. He really must have thought I was an idiot. 'What's frogs spawn?' I queried.

For once, Maurice did not explain - well, not straight away. He just burst out laughing. 'Don't you know what frogs spawn is?' he questioned between his chuckles. 'Well, it's frogs' eggs; it's like jelly, grey jelly with little black bits in it. They're the tadpoles!'

The last words were spoken with authority and made me even more confused. What on earth were tadpoles! 'Oh', I said, trying to bluff my way out. 'Yeah, tadpoles!'

Maurice must have had the patience of a Saint and no doubt realised I knew nothing about frogs and tadpoles at all. So off we went to the pond and sure enough, there it was. Frogs spawn. Great globules of the stuff all along the water's edge and still an abundance of female frogs laying more. It was fascinating.

Maurice then explained how the tadpoles hatched out, how they survived their early days of free swimming, how they then grew legs and finally became tiny frogs. I could hardly believe it. There was nothing like this in Canning Town.

There were lots of other expeditions, too, as the year progressed. Six or seven of us - Maurice, Brian, myself, Laurence and Marcel Jenkins, who lived almost opposite Blanshard's garage, and a couple of others - were rambling in the fields sandwiched between the Bow Brickhill road and the water-filled clay pit. Somebody spotted a crow's nest high in a tree and Laurence said he had never seen a crow's egg.

Maurice immediately volunteered to go up the tree to see if the nest held eggs and away he went.

Yes, there were eggs, he called down from his lofty perch, and he would bring one down. Now trying to get down a tall tree with only one free hand is no easy business, so Maurice played safe by putting the egg in his mouth so that he could descend using both hands. All went well until he was almost down, then he slipped. He gulped, we never did see the egg, but Maurice had raw crow's egg, shell and all, as a late breakfast! Nowadays, of course, and quite rightly, taking birds' eggs from nests is against the law. But all those years ago it was not illegal and most of us boys had some sort of egg collection, though perhaps not all taken in the dramatic circumstances of that particular morning!

The woods were a favourite place in summer and in those days parents had no qualms about letting us disappear into them, where we would stay all day. The sandpits in Aspley Heath woods were a great attraction and once there we would fill an empty jam jar or some other container with layers of different coloured sand to take home as mantelpiece ornaments. No day-long foray such as this was complete without bread and jam sandwiches and a bottle of water, cold tea or even fizzy lemonade if you were really lucky, and if we ran out of drink a kind old lady who lived in one of the Sandy Lane cottages close to the sandpits would draw water from her well in the garden to keep us refreshed. We loved to see the well being used and many times pretended we had nothing to drink just so that we could see her drawing up the water from underground.

On the other side of the Woburn Road, in what we called Aspley woods and where the Fullers Earth mining now takes place, there was a very deep ravine which, we were told, was the remains of an old coaching road. It must have been twenty feet or more deep and over the years trees had come down in storms to form natural bridges across the ravine. We used the trees to re-enact the legendary encounters between Robin Hood and Little John and their Norman enemies. Many a swordfight took place on the fallen tree trunks, using straight young holly saplings for our swords, though thankfully nobody ever fell into the ravine below. I hate to think how we would have explained away that sort of accident, but as children we just saw no fear.

Among my newer, sword-fencing chums was Denis Gurner, who lived with his family at 14 Downham Road, one of the unmade through roads in Woburn Sands at the time, the others being Chapel Street and Theydon Avenue.

At the beginning of the war, and throughout the conflict, the family took in a number of evacuees, though at one stage they had a rather different lodger. She was a young lady named Miss Wenham and Denis recalls she had a golden spaniel dog and a horse, called Roley, which she kept in Pratt's field - the field just behind our school off Sandy Lane.

Miss Wenham duly moved on and Denis thought no more about her time with them until the work of the wartime code-breakers at Bletchley Park began to be known. It reminded him of her stay for the family always thought at the time - but never asked because such things were not done in wartime - that she worked there.

By this time Denis was himself working for the Government and, via personnel records, attempted to trace if Miss Wenham had indeed worked at the place that was now labelled Britain's best kept secret. His diligent searches got him nowhere and it again went out of his mind until, in 1999, he watched the Channel 4 series of programmes on the Park's wartime role, entitled Station X. Soon after this his children bought him the accompanying book to the series and in the book he found a Miss Susan Wenham, one of the codebreakers, quoted four times.

Denis followed this up by writing to the book's publisher and telling of his quest to trace Miss Wenham. After a lengthy delay, obviously while the publisher consulted with Miss Wenham, Denis received a letter confirming that the lady quoted was indeed his family's wartime lodger and he was given a telephone number and an address. They corresponded and then Denis, his sister Sylvia and Miss Wenham, by then well into her eighties, met up at her home in Wiltshire.

But back to the wartime years. By this time I had lived in Woburn Sands for almost a year and was beginning to absorb ordinary, everyday rural knowledge that came almost naturally to the country children of that generation. I still felt isolated from them in some ways, especially concerning some of the clothes I wore, for while all the boys wore black boots, I still wore town shoes. Knitted balaclava helmets for boys were also beginning to make an appearance as winter drew near, but they were not to my mother's liking, so my head stayed bare. And, of course, I still had my London accent. I was the cockney kid, they were the countrymen. But I was learning.

CHAPTER 3

ACROSS THE BORDER

As the summer drew to a close and the leaves on the trees began to take on those magical colours once more, the first anniversary of our exodus from London duly arrived. It was celebrated, I remember, in the time honoured way - a drink at the pub! Mum, Dad, Uncle Jim and Aunt Vi, their children - my two younger cousins, Frances and Bob - and Gran and Grandfather Enever, settled themselves in the strip of garden at the rear of the Station Hotel. They looked back over the year and talked of the family's deliverance from the bombing as well as trying to surmise what the future might hold. The war was not going well. German U-boats were causing havoc in the Atlantic, sinking vast quantities of Allied shipping and food rationing was beginning to make life difficult. German bombers were still over London but had also attacked many other cities causing great damage. Exeter, Plymouth, Norwich, Liverpool and Coventry, where the cathedral was totally destroyed, were all prime targets.

Uncle Jim had vast experience as a merchant seaman and though he had worked at the Tate and Lyle sugar refining factory in Silvertown, close to Canning Town, for some time before the war, it was clear that he would soon be drafted on to a ship. My own father, too, expected his calling-up papers for

37

the Army at any time, for now that he did not have his own business he was no longer exempt from military service. The only reason that both father and Uncle Jim had not been called up before was their age, for both men were then well into their thirties and younger men were conscripted first. Among these were their two brothers - Jack, serving in the navy, and Bob, who was in the Army.

Such problems, however, were not in the minds of myself or my young cousins on that September evening of 1941. We chased around on the grass on our hands and knees, recreating dog racing at London's West Ham stadium and refreshing ourselves with Sparkling Special, a fizzy, raspberry sort of flavour soft drink. I can still taste it now.

Dog-racing and motor-cycle speedway were two areas of knowledge where I held sway over my new country friends. I tried to explain how the greyhounds were put into their traps, how the electrically-controlled, man-made hare was then sent round the oval track, and how the dogs were released as the hare came past to give chase. I think Maurice and the gang found it almost as rivetting as I found frogs spawn, and the same went for my deliverences on speedway.

None of them had ever seen greyhound racing or speedway before, whereas I was an old hand at both sports, going with my parents for an evening out at the dog track and with my Mum and her friends to the speedway. Both were held at the same West Ham stadium, the dog track the larger of the two ovals on the outside, the speedway track, with its red shale surface, inside that and one lap being about a quarter of a mile.

The one thing I couldn't explain about speedway though, was the particular smell that the motor-bikes seemed to leave hanging in the air as they roared past. It was some years before I learned that the smell was the exhaust fumes from the high-octane fuel that the bikes used. After the war the stadium was renamed the Terence McMillan Stadium.

School in that second year resumed its pattern under the watchful eye of Mrs Day and now that I was settled I began to enjoy the challenge of education, especially writing and the early rudiments of grammar. But school was school and enjoying life with Maurice, Brian, and the Jenkins, Farmer and Lunnon boys, the latter two families I believe living in cottages almost opposite school, was something different.

All of us would meet up at weekends to play in the recreation ground where one of the less boisterous activities would be digging for 'hog-nuts' - the round root, about the size of the pre-decimal sixpenny piece, of a small, fern-like leafed plant which I believe is a grassland weed of the yarrow family. Apparently, the roots were much loved by pigs, hence our name for them, who rooted them out of the turf with their snouts. We used old dinner knives to grub them out, the dirt was inexpertly cleaned from them with a lick of spittle and a wipe on your jersey, and into your mouth they went. The taste, as I recall, was a little bit peppery, almost like a radish a bit past its best.

It was about this time that I became aware that my parents were looking around to try and find a home of their own locally. I realise now that with the Circuitt family taking up all of the ground floor of 62 Station Road, and three lots of my own family taking up some of the top of the house, it must have been a little crowded to say the least. But the last thing I wanted was to be pitched in again to a situation where I had to make new friends and get used to a new environment. As far as I was concerned, I didn't want to go anywhere else. I was happy where I was.

I remember my parents having a long discussion on what they should do as I trailed along behind them after a blackberrying expedition on Aspley Guise golf course. Blackberries were one of the few country things I did know about, because in the past they were sometimes sold by my parents on the stall and when we visited the Kentish orchards and hopfields at about that time of the year, I had gone picking with my Gran Enever and Mum.

The Square, Aspley Guise, before the Second World War. Mr Maynard's boot and shoe repair workshop was to the rear of the cottage extreme left, which was next to the Post Office. The Courtney Memorial Hall is the A-roofed building, centre, and part of the main parade of local shops is shown left. The two-tier horse trough was removed after the war when horse drawn traffic became almost non-existent.

Mum and Dad had a sizeable basket of berries apiece, I had a jam-jar full. As we walked back to Station Road via Weathercock Lane they talked about finding a little place of their own. I was now settled at school, they said, and they didn't want to spoil that, and with my father expecting to go into the Army there seemed no point in going back to London to try and restart his business.

By the time we reached 62 Station Road their minds were made up: while Dad plied the streets with his coal cart he would make enquiries to see if there was anywhere they could rent - in those days working class families seldom bought their own houses. If it could be in Woburn Sands, because of Dad's job and me going to school, that would be fine. If not, one of the neighbouring villages, such as Wavendon, Aspley Guise or even Woburn, slightly further away, would have to do, and arrangements regarding job and school made accordingly.

October, with its leaves tumbling down and those lovely patterns of sand grains in the gutters, came and went and we were still in Station Road. It was going to be alright, I thought, we were staying put. But mid-November brought my worst fears. Dad was offered the tenancy of a cottage at the far end of Aspley Guise, about two miles away from Station Road, and we could move in a month later, just before Christmas, 1941.

Number 74, Mount Pleasant, Aspley Guise, was one of a terraced block of four cottages and it was primitive, even by the standards of those far-off days. There was no gas or electricity, although there was main drainage via the cold water standpipe in the back garden which also housed the brick built lavatory.

The cottage had two rooms on the ground floor, a small parlour-cum-living room at the front and a kitchen at the back. Both rooms were fitted with traditional open-fire ranges, complete with oven, so that they could be used for cooking. Leading off from the front room was a second door adjacent to the kitchen door which when opened revealed a flight of wooden steps leading down to a cellar. This was used for storing coal and other household goods and was also the home of a brick and concrete built copper, complete with its own hearth and chimney, which was used to do the weekly wash. Three stone steps then led upward from the cellar door to get back to ground level outside, giving access to the cold water tap with the brick-built loo beyond. The back garden then ran down to a hedge which divided it from the allotment plots, which are still in use today.

At the back of the kitchen, which sat over and above the cellar, was another door which gave access to the narrow staircase. The bottom three steps turned to the right before joining the straight run of treads which led upstairs to the two bedrooms, the larger at the front having its own fireplace, the smaller at the rear having one of its walls timber boarded which separated bedroom from stairs.

It was a far cry from Station Road where, though overcrowded, we had access to water inside the house and modern lighting available, and so different from the London flat it almost beggared belief. There we had all main services within our home, my mother being used to cooking and doing her washing with electrical appliances.

Within the scullery area in London there was a bathtub, something we hadn't clapped eyes on since we left the previous year. A bath, country style, we had soon learned on our arrival in Woburn Sands, meant a tin tub filled with hot water from kettles and pans and usually taken in front of the fire on a Friday night.

I remember my mother being more than a little

apprehensive about taking on the tenancy and not only because of the lack of facilities. It transpired that the other three tenants of the block paid four shillings a week rent - that's 20 pence in current money - but our cottage would cost us four times as much, some 16 shillings a week.

Now whether this was a bit of what we would now call discrimination, because we were city folk, not country dwellers, or whether it was a sub-let with somebody seeing the chance of making more than just a fair profit, I do not know. But in these later years the term 'rip-off' has often crossed my mind. That London taxi driver wanting ten pounds to take us to Euston with the whole of the East End pounded into twisted metal and rubble and some genuine risk involved, I can understand. But four times the normal rent in relatively ordinary, tranquil circumstances, I will never understand. However things were put right later when the four cottages were sold and the new owner, a very pleasant lady named Mrs Meadows, charged all four tenants an equal and very fair rent.

That irritant aside, my parents decided to take the plunge and we moved in two weeks before Christmas, 1941. Those winter nights were dark and long and I found the light from oil lamps difficult to get used to after living with electricity. When the lamp on the glass became warm, or even quite hot, to the touch after some time in use, you had to be careful when opening doors, especially doors leading directly outside, for the blast of cold air could easily shatter the lamp glass.

But as in life generally there were compensations. In the total darkness of my bedroom - the small one at the back of the house with its boarded wall to the stairs - I would pull back the heavy blackout curtains at the window and on a clear night just stare at the stars for hours. You can't do that in a city. The glare of street lights, the brightness of shop fronts, headlights from cars all combine to make looking beyond that pool of light to the sky very difficult. And though the blackout was in operation in London from the start of the war, the night sky didn't mean much to me then.

But now I was more than seven years old and had begun to be able to pick out some of the star constellations such as Orion's Belt and the Great Bear, which Mrs Day had explained to us at school. There were other benefits, too, from my lofty perch in that back window.

One clear January night in early 1942 I saw my first fox. He picked his way across the field at the back of the house, beyond the allotments, to a knot of trees at the summit of the rising ground which, I learned, were called 'The Clumps' by the local children.

The view of which I never tired, taken from the back window of the cottage. The Clumps are centre picture, the allotments in the foreground. The view to Woburn and its Abbey extend out of the picture to the left.

Summer and winter, day and night, I spent hours gazing from that window. To me the view from there was fabulous. In the immediate foreground and slightly to my right was a single pine tree that sprouted from the hedge that ran across the rear of the properties and made the garden boundaries.

Beyond the hedge was the footpath used by the allotment holders who gained access to their plots via a gated entrance in Gypsy Lane, the road that led out towards Woburn and which made a junction with Mount Pleasant less than a hundred yards past the front door of our new home.

The allotments were well cultivated in those days when everyone was encouraged to 'Dig for Victory' - the national slogan used to remind people to make every effort to grow their own food. After the war my father was to make those allotments his hobby, at one time tending three of the very large plots which I think run to the land measurement of some 20 poles each.

A low hedge divided the allotments from the field running up to The Clumps but behind these trees I was afforded a panoramic view of the woodland and farmland running between Aspley Guise and Woburn. In the far distance, but quite visible nestling between the trees, was Woburn Abbey, the home of the Duke of Bedford. Though it was not public knowledge at the time, buildings within the Abbey complex were being used to house 'bombe units' - machines helping to unravel the Enigma codes being broken by staff at Bletchley Park, the headquarters of the wartime Government's Code and Cypher School.

Though the interior of the cottage perhaps left much to be desired, the exterior was pleasant enough and it was that

My father, mother and grandfather Enever, who lived with us after the death of grandmother in 1946, at the door of 74 Mount Pleasant in the mid 1950s. The attractive red and black pattern of the brickwork can just be seen.

which first attracted my father. Under a slate roof punctuated by four sets of chimney stacks, the row of cottages were built in a soft, deep red brick intermingled with bricks that were a glossy coal black and contrasted beautifully. The doors to the cottages were painted dark green and each had shiny brass doorknobs. All four cottages had tiny front gardens, perhaps two or three yards square and surrounded by iron railings, with that of number 70, the first in the row, being the prettiest by far. Number 70 was the home of Mr Dick Wells and his daughter, Mrs Hooper, and her daughter Rosemary. Two more of Mr Wells' grandchildren, George and Ron Battams, also lived with their parents close by and were to become my friends.

Mr Wells was a fine athlete in his younger days and he enjoyed his garden. I remember asking him, in the summer of 1942, what were the tall flowers he grew in the front garden close to the iron railings which made up the fence? 'Phlox, my boy,' he told me. They are still one of my favourites and I love their spicey scent on a warm summer evening. But I can never seem to match the quality of blooms that Dick Wells conjured up.

The iron railings went that summer, to be melted down to make guns, tanks and bullets we were told, and were replaced by the householders with either wooden fences or posts and wire netting contraptions. Jack and Meg Grey lived at number 72, though Jack was in the Army after having been successfully lifted off the beaches at Dunkirk in June 1940, and next to us at 76 was Mrs Grey's mother, Meg Preshaw, who shared the house with her brother.

Mrs Preshaw and her brother hailed from Sunderland, in the north-east of England, and had come to the area when the depression of the mid-1930s had struck the shipbuilding industry on Tyneside. Mrs Preshaw's brother found work in the brickyards at Brogborough and at the outbreak of war they were joined by her grandson, Alan Ball, who was then living with his mother in London. Alan's older brother, Billy, was in the merchant navy and he had an older sister, Peggy.

Alan Ball was, like Maurice Circuitt, a little older than me, but there wasn't much in it and as with Maurice, I soon struck up a ready friendship with the boy everyone called 'Titch' because he wasn't very tall. But what Alan Ball lacked in inches he made up for in sporting prowess, for he was supple and stocky and seemed to have an instinctive eye for any ball game. Our friendship was to last until we were both into our early twenties - then Alan moved with his firm Lyons, the ice-cream people, from Bletchley to Preston, in Lancashire, and I haven't seen him since. From his relatives, however, I know that he is now a grandfather, just like me.

Alan must have been elsewhere on that Saturday when we moved in to the cottage because the first 'local' child that I met was his step-brother, Kenny Telford. Kenny was also living with

Alwyn (Wyn) Cook, the local carter, in Birchmoor Lane, Aspley Guise. Wyn was a familiar sight with his horse and cart around the local villages and he lived in Gypsy Lane, in the house next to the allotments. A favoured parking spot for the horse and cart was just inside the allotment gate.

Mrs Preshaw at that time but was soon to return to London, though he did appear now and then when he came to Aspley on holiday. I remember Kenny as a boy somewhat younger then me with big, soulful brown eyes and while my parents were getting organised in the cottage, he showed me the delights of exploring the thick hedge, mainly of holly, that bordered the road immediately opposite the cottages. Beyond the hedge was a collection of low-growing apple trees under which chickens clucked and scratched, with their hen-house tucked in one corner. It was a piece of land worked by Mr Alwyn Cook, usually known as Wyn, a local carter who lived not far away, just around the corner in Gypsy Lane.

Christmas came and went and I recall for us it wasn't the greatest of occasions. No electricity meant no radio, or wireless as it was then more commonly known, the only means of keeping up with the news other than the newspapers. There were non-mains radios, but my parents just never seemed to get round to getting themselves organised with one. They were powered by a device called an accumulator - a storage battery - which you had to have regularly recharged at a local garage.

The newspapers, though, told us that things were not going well. There was some limited success against the German U-boats in the Atlantic, but on land things were grim. In North Africa the German and Italian forces were pushing east toward the vital sea link of the Suez Canal, the bulk of western Europe was occupied by Germany and in the Far East, Japan had entered the war with its airborne strike against the American navy at Pearl Harbour and formed what became known as the Axis - an alliance with Germany against Britain and America. The only good news, if that was the right word but perhaps not immediately understandable to us youngsters, was that Japan's unprovoked attack had brought America into the conflict on our side. With its great industrial power there are historians who now declare that the outcome of the war was decided by that Pearl Harbour attack. With America from then on allied to Britain and its own allies and empire, ultimate victory was assured, though it would be costly and take three more years to achieve.

All of this, however, did not fill the thoughts of Alan Ball, myself, and the other children that I began to meet and know through living in Mount Pleasant. For us, our routine was simple and straightforward. Get up, go to school, come home, get out to play while it was daylight, then in and read our comics or books, listen to the radio - if you had one - then bed. At weekends, extended play, helping with odd jobs about the house and going to church or chapel took up the time spent on weekdays at school.

Though moving across the border into Bedfordshire from north Bucks, I continued to attend Aspley Heath school in Woburn Sands, even if getting to and from class was an extended affair. Initially I caught the Bedford-Aylesbury bus from the bottom of Mount Pleasant to Woburn Sands Square each morning, which cost me - and the other children from the Mount Pleasant area who were also at the same school - a penny fare. Sometimes the bus conductor would go rigidly by the rule book and want to charge twopence, because strictly speaking the penny fare only took you as far as the stop opposite Maurice Circuitt's house in Station Road, my old home. Often when this happened we would steal a march on the conductor by taking the penny fare, getting off at the bottom of Russell Street, in Woburn Sands, then running as fast

The bottom of Mount Pleasant as it is today and where it joins Bedford Road. From here we caught the bus to Aspley Heath School in Woburn Sands. The road was realigned many years ago but in the late 1940s there was a sharp kink on this corner, the carriageway being alongside the gates shown and taking the space where the grass banking is now placed. A large cedar tree, under which we sheltered when it rained, stood just inside the gated area. Old thatched cottages stood on the site of the house being built and were demolished soon after the war.

50

The Old School in School Lane, Aspley Guise, a beautiful solid structure built in local sandstone. Note the housing for the school bell high on the front facing gable. Though still known as School Lane to many, the road is now officially Woburn Lane.

as we could up Russell Street, into the High Street and thence to school. More often than not the bus still beat us by a short head, but not before we had made faces and shouted unsavoury words to the conductor as it overtook us in the High Street, close to school.

The homeward journey gave no such problems. We finished school at 3.45pm and the next bus home was not until after five o'clock. Whatever the weather, the only way to get home was to walk, a journey of almost two miles to Mount Pleasant.

Not all of the village children went to Aspley Heath. In School Lane - now Woburn Lane - Aspley Guise, Alan Ball and other Mount Pleasant area youngsters - among them Malcolm Deacon, Frank Walsh and several others who were to become friends and acquaintances - attended what was known as the Old School, as opposed to the New School, then recently built in Spinney Lane and which is still in use today. The Old School is now used as a light engineering works.

As my circle of friends began to grow so did my knowledge of country life. Maurice Circuitt and I were still good friends but now, perhaps sadly, only during school hours.

Now my mentors were Frank Walsh, Alan, Malcolm Deacon, his somewhat quieter and studious next door neighbour Peter Leigh Lancaster, and another natural sportsman, John Jackson, who lived in Bedford Road. I felt special at that time to be accepted into what was known as 'the Frank Walsh gang' for I was the baby of the group. I never recall this being a disadvantage though, in the sense of being picked upon by the others because I was the youngest or made to do their bidding. In fact, quite the reverse. They seemed to go out of their way to make me welcome and keep an eye on me. Whether it was because of my Blitz experience or what,° I don't know, but whether it was bird nesting, tree climbing, playing cricket or football or the very daring apple scrumping, I was always included. Frank lived with his family at the bottom of San Remo Road, off Mount Pleasant, and like the Preshaws, his father had found work in the brickyards after leaving his native Oldham, in Lancashire, during the depression.

As the summer of 1942 beckoned my father changed jobs, leaving Franklins to go labouring at Husborne Crawley where, close to the railway and what is now the M1 junction, a fuel depot for aviation spirit was being constructed, complete with an underground pipeline to take the fuel direct to the Cranfield airstrip some five miles away. It was in the mud and clay of the emerging depot - later to be called 'the petrol dump' by us all - that one morning my mother handed Dad his calling up papers. They had been delivered by post after he had gone to work.

CHAPTER 4

GOOD TIMES AND BAD

My father's calling-up papers told him he had to report to a training battalion at Warrington, in Lancashire, and I recall him telling me and mother that 'this was the real thing; no more being a part-time soldier.' By that he meant the few months he had spent as a member of the Aspley Guise Home Guard, who met regularly in the yard of The Bell pub, in Aspley Square, for drill, basic weapon training, map reading and the like. Though we children were not allowed to go anywhere near The Bell yard on these occasions, the presence of the Home Guard unit made the sight of khaki uniforms commonplace and the Home Guard's rifle practice on a Sunday morning in the sand pit in Mill Lane, off Salford Road and beyond the church, an event never to be missed.

The men used .22 rifles for practice in this local sand pit and when they finished - conveniently, I later realised, at a little before noon, the time when the pubs opened - we boys would dig into the sand to find the spent bullets. Lucky the lad who happened to dig where a good shot had fired, for all the bullets would be grouped close together. We used the spent bullets for all sorts of things but not least for catapult ammunition if we ever got near enough to an unsuspecting rabbit. Rabbit meat was much more widely eaten then than it is now and a classic country dish was rabbit pie. We also found them useful as lead weights on fishing lines but for this the bullets had to be chopped down in size.

When father duly went off to Warrington it left the care of the garden at the back of the cottage to Mum and me. Dad had begun to create a flower garden in the area nearest the house but a sizeable chunk at the end nearest the allotments was given over to the chicken run.

Rationing was now at its height and all manner of foods were scarce. Items like sugar, rice and tea were in very short supply, even more so since Japan had entered the war and gained notable victories in the Far East. The ration of cheese per person a week was something like two ounces - approximately 50 grams - though it was increased in the summer of 1942 to eight ounces a week. Meat, dried and canned fruit, sugar, syrup, condensed milk, canned vegetables and breakfast cereals, bacon, butter, cooking fats and eggs (one per person per week) were all rationed, so the ration book was just about the most important thing you

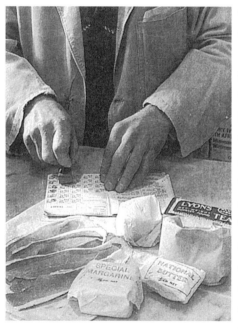

A grocer stamps coupons in a ration book to show that the ration of that item had been taken. During the war nobody starved, but the range of foodstuffs on offer was severely restricted.

owned. Virtually everything you needed to buy in the way of foodstuff was rationed, and to get your supply you had to produce your ration book for the shopkeeper to cross off or cut out the ration coupons accordingly. The more householders could produce for themselves, therefore, the better fed they would be, so many people set to keeping chickens in their back gardens for a supply of eggs and for poultry meat when the chicken's egg-laying days drew to an end. Hence our chicken run. Rabbit hutches also became a familiar back garden sight. Wild rabbits didn't just give themselves up!

There were three colours of ration book. Buff for an adult, blue for us children under 14, and green for the under-5s. Potatoes and bread were not rationed, nor was fish, but with grain having to be imported from the United States, and therefore having to run the gauntlet of the U-Boat campaigns, it was not long before white bread was replaced by a 'national wheatmeal' loaf that looked decidedly grey in colour. Not that the healthy appetite of a rising eight-year-old worried much about its looks!

With this sort of austerity all around us I learned very quickly in 1942 how to look after the chickens. With grain unobtainable they were fed on a diet of unpeeled boiled potatoes which were roughly mashed before a cheap sort of bran was mixed with the mash. Added to this was a couple of spoonsful of something called 'Karswood poultry spice' which you bought in a packet. It was a sort of orange-red powder and supposed to do something to the chickens - I know not what - which encouraged them to lay. Well lay they did, so much so that under the tuition of neighbours, my mother was able to preserve a bucketful of them in a cloudy white liquid I think was called 'eisenglass', or something like that, which kept us going through the period when the chickens were not laying so well. To this day I still think one of the nicest little things in life is that feeling you get when you take a chicken's egg warm from the nest.

As well as the potato mash, which of course had to be cooked on one of the cottage ranges in a big, black pot and which you could smell, I always thought, even outside the house, we fed the chickens on any other household scraps we thought suitable. In addition they had chickweed from the garden and later, cabbage leaves and the like when we began our small vegetable plot.

·· every available piece of land must be cultivated

GROW YOUR OWN FOOD

supply your own cookhouse

A wartime Ministry of Agriculture poster extolling everyone to grow their own food wherever possible.

I stress here that although my father's experience of life had instilled in him the ability to grow things in the ground, my mother and I really hadn't a clue. But again the neighbours were helpful and showed us the rudiments so that before long we were beginning to do quite nicely with our own potatoes, cabbages - though the white butterflies were a nuisance, or more correctly, their caterpillers were - beetroot, carrots, peas and the most rewarding of the lot, runner beans. Those early attempts at vegetable growing, I now realise, laid the foundations of the allotment gardening I now enjoy so much.

I did miss fresh fruit though. Not apples and pears, which we could buy, or on occasions, scrump from nearby orchards, but things like oranges, peaches, grapes and above all, bananas and pineapples. With my father a regular buyer in Covent Garden, Spitalfields and Stratford wholesale produce markets when we lived in London, we never went short of imported fruits. Now they were just non existent and there were days when I just longed for their different tastes.

With my father away and everyone ever conscious of rationing and, on a wider plane, of course, the progress of the war itself, I remember 1942 as perhaps the worst year of the conflict. The second year of the war, 1940, was bad enough, with

Rationing did not stop birthday parties. Sally Smith, an assistant in the shop of Aspley newsagent Mr Tripp, cuts her birthday cake watched by a seated Audrey Griffin (now Redford), Jean Pirie and Enid Phipp (now Thompson), front left. Alan Ball and Les Page are behind the girls. Ron Templeman is the older boy looking down, with his grandmother the lady on the extreme right.

the loss of Dunkirk and ultimately all of France, the Battle of Britain and the Blitz, of which many of us had first hand experience. But in 1940 there was still a general feeling, I think, that the war wouldn't last long and that things would quickly get back to normal. But it just didn't work out like that. We were now into the third year of conflict and although we now had the United States with us, things were still not going well. In North Africa we first seemed to make headway, then were pushed back east along the Mediterranean coast, Europe was firmly under the heel of the Nazi jackboot, in the Far East Singapore came under siege, Hong Kong was already lost and the U-Boats and German bombers were still exacting a heavy toll on our shipping and cities.

Worse was to come. The chickens stopped laying and the preserved eggs in the bucket were used up! Like many other children, I was about to make the acquaintance of dried egg!

Dried egg was reconstituted egg in the form of a yellow powder imported from the United States in vast quantities. I think it was claimed that it would do what any normal egg would do but, of course, you can't boil powder. Certainly it was used in cake making and such but for eating directly the best way was scrambled. Even this had its drawbacks, for if for some reason it wasn't served and eaten immediately, as it cooled down it tended to congeal and what little taste there was in it quickly disappeared. But it was not only on the food front though that people faced austerity. Clothes were also rationed.

Clothes had been on ration since 1941 but in 1942 the Government brought in regulations which laid down basic standards for everyday garments. For example, a man's jacket could not be double breasted, because this obviously used more material, there was to be no more than three pockets to a pair of trousers and zips could not be used.

The same sort of controls governed ladies' and girls' garments and 1942 saw the introduction of what were known as 'Utility' clothes. The term 'futility' did not mean that the clothes were made from old rags or that sort of thing, but it did regulate the quality of cloth as decreed by Government, who also regulated the prices that could be charges. Indeed price controls across all types of commodities, including food, were commonplace and all added to that sense of austerity. But if you were down in the dumps and actually complained about rationing you got little sympathy. The usual reply was: 'Stop moaning! Don't you know there's a war on!'

However, in the true spirit that generally prevailed in the country at that time, there were brighter things to remember as well. Not least of these for us in the four cottages was that mains electricity was laid on.

At long last the oil lamps were put away to gather dust on a shelf in the cellar and once the blackout curtains had been pulled at night you could wander from room to room flooding the place with light at the flick of a switch. We all felt better once that source of power was made available though you had to make sure you had a constant supply of shilling (5p) coins available, for the electricity was only there if you paid for it directly by feeding the meter that was housed in a small cupboard in the front room.

The electricity also gave us the chance to have what mother called 'a proper wireless.' One of the few things salvaged from the London flat was a large radio receiver made, I recall, by a company called McMichael. By today's standards it was a massive piece of kit, powered as were all radios then by valves. Some two feet wide and nearly eighteen inches high, it stood on a small table in the corner of the kitchen and became one of the mainstays of life. Television for the general public was still some years away, for what limited TV transmissions there were in the late 1930s were curtailed when war became reality.

The radio news bulletins, notable at 7am and 8am in the morning, at lunchtime and at 6pm and 9pm, kept us informed as to the progress of the war. Obviously the news content was watched over carefully by Government should the reporting of some military disaster sap morale or cause panic, but by and large the BBC recorded a balanced account and the bulletins were avidly listened to not only in the United Kingdom but in secret by the French, Dutch, Belgian and Danish civilians if they thought they could get away with it. If caught by the German occupiers it often meant internment in prison or a concentration camp and, on occasions, even death.

Backing up the all-important news bulletins were a wide range of programmes ranging from classical concerts and recitals, discussion programmes, talks on health matters by 'The Radio Doctor', hints on home-making in such austere times and above all, the comedy programmes. Head and shoulders above the rest in this area was ITMA (It's That Man Again) starring Tommy Handley.

ITMA was perhaps the first radio programme to introduce and promote the catch-phrase. 'TTFN' (Ta-ta for now) was regularly used by the characters and Mrs Mopp, Handley's cleaner in the script, would introduce herself with the sound of a door being opened and the words: 'Can I do you now, Sir?' Then there was Mona Lott, who grumbled and whinged incessantly but always told Handley, as she signed off: 'It's being so cheerful as keeps me going!' Listening to ITMA was equivalent to watching today's television soap operas such as Coronation Street, Eastenders and Emmerdale. It became a way of life and the programme was ably supported by other comedy shows featuring Arthur Askey and Richard Murdoch (Band Waggon), the Americans Ben Lyon and Bebe Daniels, who had settled in London, alongside Vic Oliver (Hi Gang) and one of my own favourites, 'Happidrome'.

'Happidrome' starred Robby Vincent, Harry Korris and Cecil Frederick as Mr Lovejoy, Ramsbothom and Enoch. Young Enoch was always getting into mischief and the show spawned another catchphrase: 'Take him away, Ramsbotham!' The programme always finished with a musical chorus, led by Mr Lovejoy: 'We three, in Happidrome; Working for the BBC; Rambotham, and Enoch, and me!' And then, of course, there was Children's Hour, which went out every evening during the week at about five o'clock and was masterminded by a wonderful man named Derek McCulloch.

'Uncle Mac', as he was known to all children, became director of Children's Hour in 1938. He had served in the First World War, where he suffered lung damage and lost an eye, and in a car accident later, lost a leg. But his indomitable spirit kept him going and during the war years he came up with a whole raft of programmes within the Children's Hour slot that were both interesting and entertaining. One of these, for the very younger listener, was 'Toytown' where he read several of the parts himself, especially that of Larry the Lamb. But he will perhaps be best remembered for adding just one word to the

'Goodnight, children' farewell at the end of the programme. It became 'Goodnight, children; everywhere.' The word everywhere seemed somehow to pull us all together, whether we were village dwellers in the country, evacuees in strange homes, kids in bombed cities or even those in more dire straits, such as orphans. It seemed to sum up the man's understanding of children's needs and his compassion. Uncle Mac died in 1967 at the age of 70.

The summer of the year, however, brought both good times and bad, as far as I was personally concerned. The bad was that my father came home on embarkation leave, prior to sailing for North Africa to become part of General Montgomery's famous Eighth Army, so it now became very clear that we wouldn't being seeing him for some time. Of course, because of security restrictions, he didn't know where his unit was being sent but he guessed North Africa and some weeks later his first letter home confirmed his initial thoughts. We now knew that he was in an active theatre of war and my mother joined the ranks of millions of other wives facing the same worries over the wellbeing of the menfolk.

The good side of things, well, to a small boy, anyway, was that when father came home on that leave he brought his Army issue Lee Enfield rifle with him. I remember him showing me how to pull the butt into my shoulder as I lay on the floor of the front room of the cottage, how to take aim through the adjustable rear sight and line up the foresight accordingly, how to work the bolt mechanism that fed the .303 ammunition from the magazine into the breach and how to change the magazine. Needless to say, the rifle was not loaded, but that didn't stop mother tut-tutting as bit about me being too young

Church Hill, Aspley Guise, a range of modern houses built on the site of Rev. Harry Clothier's rectory where we met for cubs.

to play with guns. None of us realised that just over ten years into the future, I would have my own Lee Enfield issued to me as a young National Service recruit.

The other good thing was that in August I reached the magical age of eight, magical because it meant I could now join the cubs.

The Aspley Guise cub pack was run by the village Rector, the Rev. Harry Clothier, and met on Saturday morning at about ten o'clock for two hours, or sometimes a little longer, at the rectory, opposite the church in Salford Road. The rectory was approached by a winding, uphill drive, which led to its front door. The rectory was demolished some years ago and the ground where the drive, building and its garden stood is now called Church Hill, the site of a small cul-de-sac of pleasant houses.

I found Rev. Clothier to be an affable, kindly man, assisted in the running of the cub pack by a lady from Aspley Hill, Woburn

Sands, named Winnie Pearce. My first morning there was in company with Alan Ball, who being that bit older was already a member, and lots of other village lads that I knew, including Les Page, who lived in Bedford Road. I don't know if things are different now, but in those days the pack was broken down into 'sixes' - that number of cubs to a team - and Les at that time was my 'sixer' or team leader.

I joined in readily enough with all the various activities whilst at the same time being briefed by Harry Clothier and to some extent, Les, on what uniform I would need to wear and where it could be purchased. In the event I think my first outfit, including the distinctive green cap with its yellow piping, came to me second-hand. Over the ensuing weeks I found my favourite pastime was tracking and fieldcraft and the initial tutoring by Maurice Circuitt and others in matters country began to take on broader dimensions.

Let me cite just one example. When I first came to Woburn Sands, nearly two years earlier, I had no idea that the crow family of birds comprised several different species, including, of course, the rook. It was Maurice Circuitt and my Woburn Sands friends who put me right.

There were plenty of rooks around in those days and they were often shot by farmers to deter other members of the rook colony, or rookery, from raiding the newly sown cornfields. The favoured nesting place for rooks is in the topmost branches of tall trees adjoining such fields though in this day and age the ravages of Dutch elm disease some years ago, coupled with modern farming methods of grubbing out hedgerows and trees, has given the rook a hard time in finding such sites. They build their nests early in the year - often as early as February- and congregate the nests together to create the rookery. The nest is built mainly of twigs and at times raiding of other nests takes place to get what seems to be the best twigs.

The reason the rook likes to be near cultivated land at nesting time is not, though, purely so it can steal the seedcorn. It is because young rooks, when they hatch, are fed on an exclusive diet of worms and grubs. The early nesting means that cultivated land is still often damp from winter and early spring rains so there is an abundance of such food to be found.

After the eggs are laid, and depending on the vagueries of incubation, the rook chicks obviously hatch out at different times. The strongest of these will take the most worms and many young rooks never make it beyond the nest as, under nourished, they get weaker and die. The diet only changes as the young rook gets older. So the farmer shot rooks not just because adult rooks were taking the seedcorn, but because they were disturbing the sowings in their efforts to find worms and grubs to feed their young. The whole colony taking the sprouting corn for food came some weeks later. Those fieldcraft sessions at cubs added to Maurice Circuitt's teachings and improved my knowledge of rural life immensely.

As I progressed in the cubs I became a 'seconder', which meant I was now Les's deputy and allowed to wear a single, narrow, yellow armband denoting that rank. Les wore two bands as a sixer, as I did later myself, and then came the most senior position in the pack, that of 'senior sixer' which, when I was later accorded that position, gave me the privilege of wearing three bands and leading the pack in our opening and closing chanted chorus, the 'grand howl.'

Some of the Aspley Guise cubs in the summer of 1943. Among the boys pictured are, back row, left to right: Tim Fryer, Malcolm Deacon, Gerald Beale, John Pirie, John Cox, Les Page, John Jackson, Peter Leigh-Lancaster, Denis Gurner; front: not known, Denis Cox, Mervyn Hemmings, Alan Ball, Ted Enever, Malcolm Posner, not known.

Cubs, however, became only a part of pleasant Saturdays, for the afternoon was often spent at one of the two cinemas nearby, The County, at Fenny Stratford and The Studio at Bletchley.

Alan Ball and I soon had the routine down to a fine art. We would finish cubs and then kill time, if we had to, by climbing the various trees in and around the Clothiers' garden. A holly tree right by the roadside and flanking the drive where it turned sharply up towards the rectory was a favourite, and is still there today. Then, a little after 12.30pm, we would watch for the spry figure of my mother emerging from the iron gateway of The Close, the field that formed a large wedge of land between Salford Road and Bedford Road and which provided a short cut between the two by virtue of a public footpath. The Close was something of a famous wartime landmark in the village, being the spot where a German bomber dropped its stick of bombs in 1940. No-one was hurt but there was damage to property and the incident is recorded in more detail in Chapter 5.

When mother appeared we knew lunch was on hand, for she would bring us a sandwich of something, usually corned beef or hopefully my favourite, fried sausage, which would still be warm from the pan. Alan and I would munch away as the three of us, and other villagers and children, made our way down Salford Road to the station to catch the two-carriages motor train, as it was known, to Fenny Stratford or Bletchley.

Whichever cinema we chose we invariably left the train at Fenny Stratford. The County was close by, on the Watling Street and only some fifty yards or so from the Watling Street bridge entrance to the station. The Studio sat roughly halfway between Fenny and Bletchley station, on the site which is now modern offices and next to the Bletchley Arms, and was possibly the more comfortable of the two cinemas, the County being a little more cramped. This was the heyday of the cinema and the places were always full. Then, after the show, we would make our way back to Fenny station, sometimes stopping at the British Restaurant, now the Masonic Hall, close to the junction of Victoria Road and what is now Queensway, then Bletchley Road, in Bletchley.

The British Restaurants were run by the local authorities and subsidised by Government. They operated on the lines of a self-service canteen and served meals and snacks that were both plentiful and cheap. For about a shilling (5p) you could buy a meal of meat, potatoes, cabbage and gravy.

CHAPTER 5

BOMBS AND MEMORIES

Looking back to those early days at Woburn Sands, I now realise that in September 1940 I thought I was pretty unique. I was, after all, a city kid dumped somewhat unceremoniously into a new way of life in the country. But within a few days of starting at Aspley Heath school, I realised I wasn't unique at all.

In my class was a lad named Pat Walters who hailed from Forest Gate, not far from my own native Canning Town. Pat was one of five Walters children - Joan, Betty, Tony, himself and younger sister Jill. Joan, the eldest, was a member of the Women's Territorial Army in 1939 and was called up immediately into the ATS when it was clear that war was imminent. The other four children were evacuated from Forest Gate by the local authority on Friday 1 September 1939, two days before war was declared. Tony was sent to Oxfordshire, the others to Thetford, and they were apart for about six months. Then their father, Ernie Walters, who was a barber and gents hairdresser, took a job with George Wesley, who owned a hairdressing salon in the High Street, Woburn Sands. With the job went a house, number 14 High Street, opposite Russell Street. It meant the family, other than Joan in the ATS, could be reunited and they were in their new home by March, 1940.

Betty was by now of school leaving age and joined the local

electrical engineering firm run by Cyril Hutton. The company had shop premises in the High Street. Tony, Pat and shortly after, Jill, who I remember as a pretty girl with a mass of blonde curls, began to attend Aspley Heath school.

Tony now lives in Bletchley, not far from me, and recalls the day the bombs were dropped at Aspley Guise. It was getting on for midday on a murky Friday in the late autumn of 1940 and with the other senior boys of the school - Tony was then about 13 - he was being put through 'Exercises', or what we might now call physical training, by his teacher, Mr Cooper, in the boys playground that fronted the Woburn Road. There was the

Bob Page, nearest camera right, is part of the village scout guard of honour at the wedding of their assistant scout master, Frank Hodgkinson, at St Botolph's church, Aspley Guise, on 25th September 1942, when he married Lilian Brown, of Banbury. Frank, who was then 37 and in the RAF, was an artist in civilian life and was billeted with the Clothiers at the rectory. He was stationed at nearby Cranfield. Other boys in the picture are Malcolm Munn, furthest from camera, right, and on the left, Claude Lees and John West, later to become brothers-in-law when Claude married John's sister, Jackie.

sound of aircraft engines and the boys looked up to see a Dornier bomber just about to unload its bombs. They saw them fall away towards Aspley Guise, heard the muffled explosions, and were promptly sent home for the day by Mr Cooper! At about the same time as this scare, Ernie, Tony's father, joined the Woburn Sands Home Guard and spent his first duty sitting on Aspley Guise golf course scouring the skies for German parachutists. None, of course, ever came, but as I have mentioned earlier, the fear of invasion was still in people's minds at that time.

Malcolm Deacon, with several other boys, was on his way home from the Old School that lunchtime to where he lived with his mother and younger sister, Pamela, at 64, Mounty Pleasant. Malcolm was rising seven years-old and his father, Ralph, was in the army, a corporal with the Beds and Herts Regiment.

The boys' route took them along Spinney Lane, which runs parallel to the Bedford Road, and across the separating field the youngsters spotted a convoy of army lorries. Keen to see more, they ran across the field toward the lorries. As they neared Bedford Road, the Dornier appeared, unloaded its bombs and in all probability tried to strafe the convoy with machine gun fire. Malcolm remembers seeing the ground in front of him erupt in a series of small spurts, which he and the other boys laughed at, thinking it was a huge joke. Shrapnel from the bomb casings was unlikely to have dropped in a straight line, but strafing machine gun bullets would. What now seems highly likely is that the a gunner in the Dornier was a some yards off his target of the lorries but very nearly machine gunned the young boys.

Bob Page, the elder brother of my cub sixer, Les, was also on his way home from school when the Dornier came over their house, number 10, Bedford Road. The house was among the closest properties to the actual explosions.

Bob heard the explosions, rushed home to make sure his pet rabbit was alright, but found it dead in its hutch. Bob thinks it died from the shock of hearing the shriek of bombs.

Number 15, Bedford Road, the home of Jim Broadbent and on the opposite side of the road to the Pages' home, was the nearest property to where the first bomb in the stick of five actually fell. The bomb came down inside The Close but near to the hedge that bordered the road and to the west, that is The Square side, of the memorial that stands on Bedford Road in front of Aspley House. Mrs Eleanor Allen's nanny was out with the two Allen children in a pram close by in Bedford Road at the time. Neither she nor the children were hurt but she was badly shaken and the children and pram covered in dirt from the blast. Mrs Allen - later Lady Allen, the wife of Sir Kenneth and whose home was The Manor in Salford Road - was the evacuee billeting officer.

The blast also rippled the slates on the roof of the Broadbent's house, leaving a sizeable hole as well as doing some other minor damage. For the rest of the war Jim Broadbent and his family lived with a tarpaulin on the roof covering the hole but it didn't keep out the weather completely and some interior walls became damp after a time and sprouted fungus.

Other properties in the village reported windows smashed by the blast of the bombs, all of which fell across The Close, and at 12, Salford Road, the home of the Cullip family, a door at the top of the stairs was blown off its hinges. Mrs Cullip had not long given birth to her youngest child, Trevor, and was down-stairs at the time , but June, her elder daughter who told me the story, relates that the family cat was upstairs when the bombs dropped and whether that survived the shock or not she didn't know!

As the Dornier passed over Aspley Heath and opened its bomb doors Sid Randall, the brother of the headmistress of the New School, Miss Randall, was chatting in Sinfield's builders yard, just to the rear and side of The Bell pub, to Pastor Charles Davis of the church that met in the Courtney Memorial Hall in The Square. The Pastor was on his way home and was carrying a wooden clothes-line prop at the time.

Sid, Sinfield's manager, was a 1914-18 war veteran and, like Pastor Davis, was a special constable. The Pastor threw himself to the ground as they spotted the plane while Sid merely asked: 'What are you doing down there?'

'We're b-b-being bombed!' the Pastor exclaimed. When excited or under stress he tended to stammer.

'Well, they won't hit us,' said Sid, drawing on his military experience and gauging correctly the trajectory of the bombs as they left the plane. 'They'll drop over in The Close; we'll be alright.' He was right in his assumption and the next morning Sid's eight years-old son, Chris, was in The Close collecting what bits of bomb casing he could find.

Along with the village policeman, Pc 'Bobby' Banks, who lived in Mount Pleasant, the special constables handled all sorts of wartime duties, not least the guarding of aircraft which crashed nearby. Early in the war a Hampden bomber came down at Husborne Crawley, the next village to Aspley Guise, bursting into flames and killing some of the crew.

The pilot and navigator, so the story goes, parachuted to safety but got caught up in the surrounding trees. They were cut down by a land girl. For the next few days the special constables were on hand guarding the burnt out wreckage, the only recognisable part left being the twin tailplane. The wreckage itself was finally cleared up by Italian prisoners of war based at The Holt, one of whom took it upon himself to become Malcolm Deacon's mentor. When the POWs were marched off to the scene of the crash Malcolm was with his new friend and some of the other village boys. The youngsters were not allowed anywhere near the scene, however, until the bodies of the crash victims were recovered.

Later in the war the wooded area behind the Duke of Bedford's estate wall at Husborne Crawley saw more than one Stirling bomber caught up among the trees as it failed to negotiate the emergency airstrip within the grounds of Woburn Abbey. The police and specials, I remember, did once turn a blind eye when several of us from Mount Pleasant raced down Horsepool Lane to the area and clambered all over an aircraft which had finished up nose first at the base of a tree.

On another occasion Malcolm, Norman 'Polly' Walsh, Frank's younger brother, my next door neighbour Alan Ball and some others - but not me, so I don't know what I was up to - grabbed their bikes to get to the scene of another crash.

A Wellington twin-engined bomber had come down in a field close to where the Junction 13 interchange on the M1 motorway now stands and not far from the petrol dump site. To their surprise there were no guards and they clambered over the wreckage and made souvenirs of spent canon shells, machine gun bullets and small percussion caps. They thought it great fun throwing the percussion caps onto the road as they rode home, the caps making a lively bang as they exploded.

Some time after this escapade Malcolm was around the bottom of Mount Pleasant on foot when several half-track vehicles, either Bren gun carriers or light tanks, came through the village. As they passed by Mount Pleasant a container fell from the back of one and went unobserved by the crew, though young Master Deacon spotted it. Thinking it could be important, he picked it up and trekked all the way to Woburn Sands Square with his heavy load where he caught up with the half-tracks at rest. Malcolm duly handed over his container, firmly believing he had saved some precious petrol, only to be thanked but told it wouldn't really have mattered about its return because it only contained water!

His disappointment was somewhat tempered by having the opportunity to look at the half-tracks close up, and he was so fascinated by the large steel drive wheels that he touched the shiny metal. That was a mistake, for the wheels were extremely hot and he burnt the palm of his hand! I suppose in today's language we would call that a double whammy!

Aspley Guise took in its first evacuees on the same day that Tony Walters said goodbye to his two sisters and brother in Forest Gate - Friday 1st September, 1939. The Aspley evacuees came from another east London district, Walthamstow, and like the Walters, were moved under the direction of their local authority. Some journeyed to the village via Euston and Woburn Sands, others came on the St Pancras line to Ampthill and were then bussed to the Parish Hall where Mrs Allen was there to allocate them to various

The Parish Hall, Aspley Guise, the spot where the Wathamstow evacuees were brought on 1st September 1939. From here they were allocated to families by Mrs Allen, the billeting officer.

families after distributing little parcels of fruit and sweets.

Among them was ten years-old Sam Beasley who had arrived via Ampthill and the bus with his older sister, Olive. Sam was a pupil at the Primary School in Pretoria Avenue, Walthamstow, and his first recollection of the village was the two-tiered horse trough in The Square, the top trough for horses, the lower for dogs. He and Olive were billeted with the Clothiers at the Rectory where every member of the household - Rev and Mrs Clothier, the Clothier's two children, Peter and Flora, and the two Beasley evacuees - had their

A young Sam Beasley, who was destined to grow up in nearby Salford.

75

own small sugar bowl. Their sugar ration was put into the bowl at the start of the week so everyone was responsible for their own amount.

Later, early in 1941, Sam's parents had a close call when the blast from a direct hit on their neighbours' Anderson took out their home. The neighbours were killed and the Beasleys came to Aspley Guise where Harry Clothier converted a garage for them to live in.

After about six months the family was able to rent Mill Farm house at nearby Salford from the farmer, Mr Summerford, and it remained their home until long after the war.

On the day Sam came to Aspley Guise, six years-old Iris Sullivan was evacuated from Bow to Banbury with her brother, later to be joined by her mother when she was bombed out. The family had relatives at Brogborough so the Sullivans moved from Banbury to be with them. Some years later Sam and Iris met at Brogborough Club and were married in the early 1950s. They now live in Tattenhoe, Milton Keynes, after spending 47 years at Brogborough.

Another of the Walthamstow evacuees was Billy Blowes, who, like Sam and me, was destined to make the district his home. Billy and his brother were taken to Euston by their mother after being told they were going for a holiday in the country. Like Sam, Billy was ten-years-old and could hardly wait for the train to arrive. From Woburn Sands the boys and their Walthamstow friends were taken to Aspley Guise Parish Hall by bus where they were lined up outside and identified by the labels on their lapels.

Billy and his brother were taken to Rosemary Cottage, number 48, Mount Pleasant, the home of Mr and Mrs Bill

Billy Blowes, pictured in the garden of Mr and Mrs Fowler at Rosemary Cottage, Mount Pleasant, in the summer of 1940.

Fowler. Mrs Fowler - Elsie Fryer before she married Bill - was an accomplished musician and gave piano lessons to local children, me among them, as well as being organist and Sunday School teacher at the Mount Pleasant Methodist chapel, next to The Wheatsheaf pub, kept by Mrs Amy Long. The chapel building is now a private house.

There were roses round the door of Rosemary Cottage, Billy recalls, and he was shown to a pleasant back bedroom where he looked out to be captivated, as I was two years later, by that stunning view. He remembers particularly seeing sheep in The Clumps field, and was fascinated by the backdrop of fir trees beyond, never having seen fir trees before.

Billy quickly settled with the Fowlers to enjoy a happy childhood and, under Elsie's guidance, he sent a postcard home to his mother in Walthamstow. It read:

'Dear Mum. We arrived safely and we are living in a pleasant home. We have just had our tea and are now going out.'

Young Billy certainly enjoyed his food and remembers most

meals contained meat of some sort. But best of all, lunches or cooked evening meals always consisted of two courses, or 'afters' as Billy's London speech would have it. Suet puddings in the form of spotted dick or ginger puddings were a particular favourite and within a year he had put on a stone or more in weight.

Like the other evacuees in the village Billy Blowes went to the Old School in School Lane, where Miss Curle was the headmistress, ably assisted by Mr George Petifer and a Mr Newton, who, the boys found, could cane quite hard if you misbehaved. The teachers were strict, Bill remembers, but thinks it was for the evacuees own good, as being strangers to the country way of life, the teachers did not want them going astray.

For the young Walthamstow boy, poaching was not 'going astray' because most of his country classmates knew how to make and set a snare to take the occasional rabbit. So Bill set about the same task and for the first couple of days caught nothing. Then one day after school - success. Long before my time, Billy Blowes was learning the country crafts!

Many other families in Aspley Guise were to take in evacuees throughout the war years, among them the Cullip family in Salford Road and the Povey family, who lived in Duke Street.

June Cullip - now Mrs June Horne and living in Stony Stratford - remembers how two young girls came to them in a shocking state. They were dirty and unkempt and wet themselves continuously, often taking off their underclothes and hiding them during the day so that they would not get soaked. As well as all this they were generally badly behaved kids and gave Mrs Cullip something of a hard time. At the opposite end of the scale was an older lady known to the Cullip's as Gran Cordall and she stayed with them for a long time.

Mary Povey was seven years-old when war was declared. The daughter of a well known Aspley man, Tom Povey, the water engineer and manager of the local Drainage and Water Supply Joint Committee, Mary - now Mary Manning and living in Woburn Sands - recalls that evacuees came to live with them in their Duke Street home early in the war and in total they housed seven throughout the course of the conflict. These included the Burnett brothers from Walthamstow, whom Tom took to Bedford to buy them new clothes.

Mary remembers filling sandbags to protect against potential blast damage by going to the long since disused sand pit in Woburn Lane, close to her father's Birchmoor works, and nights spent in the air raid shelter which her father built in their garden. The children loved these impromptu get-togethers for it was open house for most of those who lived in Duke Street. Everyone would join in with sing-songs and Mary was struck as a young girl by the friendliness and co-operation that was later to be called community spirit.

As well as the evacuees the Poveys also had billeted with them RAF servicemen; and in the nearby woods Mary remembers there was an army camp complete with armoured cars. Like most Aspley children of the time, she went to the Old School in School Lane.

Among the village boys at that school with Billy Blowes was Bob Page, whose rabbit died the day the bombs dropped. Bob, who was born at his Grandma's house in Mount Pleasant in

1929, can remember the Old School having very high ceilings and being a cold place, especially in winter. In these colder months the third of a pint bottles filled with milk which the children used to enjoy at morning break, or playtime as it was then called, would be brought in to stand in front of the big fireplace which most schoolrooms boasted at that time.

Certainly that was the practice at the Old School at Aspley, as it was at my Aspley Heath school at Woburn Sands, for just a few minutes in front of the fire would soon take the chill off the milk. I think we paid something like $2^1/_2$ pence (old money) a week for the milk - about a penny in current money.

Many of the windows at my Aspley Heath school were bricked up to stop the danger of flying glass causing injuries should bomb blast ever blow them out, and the Old School was given the same treatment. But Bob recalls that when he transferred to the New School when it opened in October 1940, the windows remained intact, save for sticky tape running from corner to corner, the idea being that this would hold the glass in place if it shattered.

Bob was a true country child and learned to milk a cow at the age of ten. He collected wood and fir cones from The Clumps for the fire at home and as he got older he helped on the local farms with both hay making and harvest, as did most of the village boys of that age and as I did, later. With the harvest the boys would collect up the sheaves of corn as they were cut by the binder being pulled behind its tractor and stack them into a standing bundle of sheaves known as 'stooks' so that they could ripen off and dry out before being collected by horse and cart. Once collected they were taken to the rick yard at the farm, stacked accordingly, and left until later in the year when the threshing machine would do its work in separating the individual grains from the ears of corn and the corn stalks. A modern combine harvester does the whole operation in one go.

Other memories do not have such a pleasant ring. Corporal Ralph Deacon, 5th Battalion, Beds and Herts, was stationed at Arundel Castle, in Sussex in 1941, waiting to go overseas. It was here that his wife, Dolly, and the two children, Malcolm and Pamela, visited him to say their goodbyes. Ralph was a member of the Territorial Army before the war and as soon as hostilities began he was called up.

At about that time he had bought Malcolm a toy car, complete with reversing facilities and its own garage. The garage had a telephone on the wall and when you lifted the telephone this worked a cord which opened the garage door. Pulling the back bumper of the car engaged the reversing facilities and the car backed itself into the garage. As soon as the bumper touched the back wall and was pushed in, the car stopped.

Ralph Deacon, Malcolm's father, who died at the hands of his Japanese captors in December 1942, ten months after being taken prisoner at Singapore. In November 2000, three years after the death of his widow, Dolly Deacon, the British Government awarded surviving prisoners or their widows an ex-gratia payment of £10,000 as compensation for their suffering.

Ralph and the family said their goodbyes and he set sail for Bombay in India and then on to Singapore, in the Far East. His ship docked in Singapore on the same day that the garrison surrendered and he and his companions literally walked straight off the ship into the arms of the Imperial Japanese Army to become prisoners of war. It was 15 February, 1942.

Dolly and the children heard nothing from Ralph until the next year, 1943, when a postcard arrived via the Red Cross saying he was safe and well and a prisoner. Subsequent events were to show that what the card said was probably far from true. Within a few weeks of receiving the card Dolly Deacon was informed by the War Office that her husband had died in a Japanese prisoner of war camp on 9 December 1942, some months before she had received his card, which must have travelled on a long and bureaucratic journey by the time it reached Mount Pleasant.

The simple white marker showing Corporal Deacon's army number, rank, regiment and date of death on his grave in the Far East.

On that day in 1943 when the news came through, Malcolm was already at school and my own mother, who shared the same name, Dolly, as Mrs Deacon, went along to number 64 to offer some comfort. Later, my mother was in Mount Pleasant when she saw Malcolm.

'Is your Mum alright, Malcolm,' she asked, not knowing that Malcolm was unaware of his father's death.

'Well, yes,' Malcolm answered. 'Well, I think so.'

'I think you'd better get home quick,' my mother told him as the penny dropped and she realised he had not been told of his father's death.

Malcolm ran home as fast as he could to find his mother in tears as she broke the news that he would never see his Dad again. Malcolm wept with her as she told him: 'You're the man of the house now.'

Malcolm remembered that one of his Dad's jobs was to chop wood for the fire, so as man of the house he did no more than go to straight to the shed and spend the next hour chopping a great heap of sticks. He realises now it was his way then of coming to terms with the loss. In later years he was to talk to survivors who were with his father at the time and met the man who cradled his father's head as he passed away.

George Norman was in our age group and lived at a house called Hazelmere, one of a block of three at the bottom of West Hill, and next to Nether Hall. George's father, Jack, was also with the 5th Battalion, Beds and Herts, and so, like Ralph Deacon, was due to go to India and Singapore. But he missed the draft by being on compassionate leave when his expectant wife was not too well and the baby was stillborn. Instead of going to Singapore he was later posted to Gibraltar.

Jack was a setter at the Brogborough brick works before the war and moved from one of the Brogborough estate houses to West Hill because the brickworks' fumes were aggravating young George's asthma. The house was owned by

Members of the Beds and Herts Regiment outside Woburn Sands station. The picture was taken either on the mobilisation of the Territorial Army in 1939 or later when members of this group were home on embarkation leave. Jack Norman is standing, extreme left.

their milkman, Harry Young, and one of George's earliest memories is going to the side door of the Young's dairy - the house on the corner of West Hill and Wood Lane and about fifty yards away - and collecting milk in an enamel two pint can with a wire handle. On the way back he tripped on his own front step and spilt the lot! During the war Mr Young's daughter, Dolly, would skim the cream from the milk for George to drink before she filled the can, telling him firmly: 'Now drink this all up Georgie and don't tell your Mum!' George says no wonder he grew up to be nicknamed Podge by his school chums!

He started at the Old School just before the war and remembers builders making alterations to the windows and erecting blastproof walls in front of the school entrances.

Jack Norman with young Georgie in the winter of 1939.

When the New School opened in 1940 he transferred there and collected acorns with the other children from the three big oak trees at the front of the building. These were then picked up by Wyn Cook with his horse and cart and taken to Woburn Abbey for pig food. He also recalls collecting rose hips which which were then sent away to be made into rose hip syrup, a supplement for babies.

A member of the St Botolph's church choir, George's fellow choristers volunteered him one evening to be bunked up over the wall of Aspley House to try and scrump some grapes from the conservatory. But he fell off the wall, hurt himself and cried, was duly discovered and then taken into the house where he found American and British Air Force officers enjoying drinks. He was given a bit of a lecture by a man he now knows to be Peter Calvocoressi, of Bletchley Park fame, and first aid for a grazed knee. All his choir mates had run off but George had the last laugh; the officers gave him an almost full box of chocolates which he scoffed sitting behind a brick wall in The Square, not daring to take them home and having to explain to his Mum how he came by them.

As a youngster he guessed there was something a bit different going on at next door Nether Hall when soldiers appeared and began rigging aerials. He believes now the place was part of the propaganda broadcast network. Two of the soldiers came into the family garden and ran an aerial from a large tree back into Nether Hall but to George this was not so exciting as the day his Dad came home on leave and shot a hare in the field opposite, now part of the Mount development. It was an excellent shot, George tells me, for his father qualified as a marksman in the army and the off-ration hare made a fine meal for the family.

With her special design of gas mask issued to the under 5s at the ready, Sylvia Norman, George's younger sister, poses proudly with her father in 1940. Gas masks were carried everywhere at the start of the war but by 1941, when it was clear that gas was not to be used, the habit rapidly lapsed.

A pal of George's was a lad called Billy Staley, who lived at the top of West Hill. When Billy's Dad came home on leave from the army, Billy somehow managed to 'borrow' his sten gun.

A gang of lads, or 'old boys' to use the local expression, George among them, nipped off to the nearby fields where Billy promptly squirted off a few rounds of the Sten's 9mm ammunition. How, or if, he explained that away to his father no-one seems to remember.

Billy's elder brother worked on the railway and towards the end of the war managed to get hold of some trackside fog detonators. They soon found their way into the hands of various old boys, including George, who banged a hole in his with a nail, extracted the black powder, wrapped this in paper and watched it go up in a satisfying puff of smoke when it was set fire.

Taking what he thought was now the empty detonator container into the living room of his home, he threw it on the fire. A few minutes later there was an almighty bang, the front of the grate was blown off and hot coals showered all over the room. Almost deafened by the explosion, but unhurt, George somehow managed to refit the front of the grate and collect up the hot coals, but not before one of the curtains at the French windows caught fire. George tried to conceal the evidence but, of course, his mother found out and he was soon on the receiving end of a good hiding. In our day 'spare the rod and spoil the child' was an accepted maxim but I don't think it did us any lasting harm and certainly taught us the difference between right and wrong. George can vouch for that!

George's father, Jack, survived the war and ended it as an army stevedore on the River Weser and Dortmund-Ems canal in Germany. During this time he and others of his regiment - by then he was a Royal Engineer - had to excavate the mass graves for the thousands of victims of the Belsen Concentration Camp. After he was demobilised in 1946, he would never speak about this experience.

Two years before, in 1944, the Duke Street community was in shock when it learned of the death of Howard Heald, a Lieutenant with the Dorset Regiment. Mary Manning, and two boys about my age, John Comerford and Brian Tyers, who lived next door to each other in Duke Street, remember Howard going off in his uniform to Bedford Modern School before the war.

'Jelly' Heald, as I am told he was known locally, was I believe only 21 years-old when he lost his life, and along with Ralph Deacon, was among the seven Aspley Guise men who failed to return from the conflict.

The other five were: Pte Charlie Cox, Beds and Herts, who died on 18 October 1943; Pte Reg Lawrence, Yorks and Lancs, 4 July 1944; Pte Dennis Odell, Monmouth Regt, 6 March 1945; Tom Darren, a private soldier, no exact date, but 1942; and Anthony John Wade, able-seaman, RN, 7 December 1942.

The eight Woburn Sands men who gave their lives were B. Clayton, S.K. Hardy, F.E. Hollier, J. Jackson, B. W. Lunnon, A.R. Poston, J. Shelton and W. White.

May they rest in peace and as those poignant words of Laurence Binyon remind: 'At the going down of the sun, and in the morning, we will remember them.'

CHAPTER 6

HOME FRONT SUPPORT

By 1942 the words 'home front' were being widely used to cover all the civilian activities dedicated to helping the war effort, be it the work of the munitions factories, the task of the Observer Corps in spotting enemy aircraft, the Home Guard, the efforts of the girls in the Land Army working on the farms, the role of the Women's Voluntary Service (WVS), the air raid wardens, part-time fire-fighters and fire-watchers, or the 'make-do-and-mend' regime that affected every household.

Both Woburn Sands and Aspley Guise had Auxiliary Fire Service units and my school chum Denis Gurner was once unwittingly caught up in the attentions of the Woburn Sands firemen .

On a day when Woburn Sands was staging one of its fund-raising activities for the war effort, part of the programme was a parade and a fire-fighting demonstration. Denis, then seven years-old, was out with the rest of the Woburn Sands boys and was caught misbehaving by his Dad, Bill, one of the Woburn Sands firemen. 'Home, now!' Bill told him sternly, and Denis began to retrace his steps from Station Road back to the High Street and home in Downham Road.

He had got as far as Bill Shortland's shop in the High Street when he was spotted by Bill, who was leader of the fire crew.

A patriotic parade featuring Woburn Sands youngsters early in the war. A young Denis Gurner is the soldier with the rifle shouldered on the right, two ranks behind the boys in the white sailor suits. The boy in the cap close to the front is wearing lace-up boots common to most boys for everyday wear. This parade must have been special, for on this occasion shoes seem to prevail!

The Woburn Sands fireman at the outbreak of war. Bill Shortland is standing, hand on ladder. Frank Woolett, a gents' hairdresser who worked at Wesley's shop in the High Street, is thought to be the bespectacled man at the back.

Aspley Guise Volunteer Fire Brigade

'I want you!' Bill Shortland told him. 'I can't,' said Denis. 'Me Dad's just told me to go home.' 'You can go home later,' Bill said. 'I want you up on that flat roof above my shop because we're doing a Fire Service demonstration.' Denis duly did as he was told, wandered up to the flat roof and lay down. After about ten minutes there was a great ringing of fire bells and a ladder appeared over the lip of the roof followed by a big uniformed figure. 'I thought I told you to go home!' said the fireman. It was his father, who promptly threw him across his shoulder and took him down the ladder to demonstrate a most proficient rescue.

The Aspley firemen were led by Frank Woods, senior, whose two sons, Frank and Jack, were also members of the unit as was Harry Armsden, who lived in San Remo Road and Geoff Jackson, who lived in Duke Street and was the brother-in-law of Jim Broadbent. Frank Woods, senior, appears to have been something of a character and sported enormous flat feet. An accident in his younger days, when they were crushed by a roll of lead, meant he walked very splay-footed.

The unit's headquarters were behind the Parish Hall in School Lane where its drying tower was quickly discovered by the boys as an ideal climbing frame. One of its most ardent fans was Les Page who was always in trouble for clambering all over it. Les had a good reason though, so he tells me. The tower was almost next to a Miss Bandy's garden which boasted some excellent apple trees, so the tower provided the ideal spot to pinpoint which boughs carried the best apples for the next scrumping expedition.

The firemen used some rather antiquated equipment - a tender pulled behind a lorry was about all they had - and to the best of my knowledge were not called upon for any major blaze during the war, though chimney fires were not uncommon. As an auxiliary unit before the war, however, they played their part in dealing with a major fire when they were called out to a blaze at Piers Court, a large thatched house towards the Woburn end of School Lane.

Perhaps the highest profile of the home front activity however, was enjoyed by the Home Guard, which began in the early days of the war under the title of 'Defence Volunteers' but was changed when Prime Minister Winston Churchill referred to them as the Home Guard. As with the auxiliary fire service, both villages had their Home Guard units and, as I have mentioned earlier, my father joined the Aspley Guise Home Guard early in 1942.

A year before, Jim Broadbent had joined. Now a sprightly senior citizen of some 86 years, Jim is the last surviving member of the detachment and recalls that some of their individual and joint escapades might well have come straight out of an episode of 'Dad's Army', the highly successful television series of some years ago which dwelt on actions of the mythical Warmington-on-Sea Home Guard in the 1940s.

Born at the beginning of the First World War in 1914, Jim

The men of Woburn Sands Home Guard parade through the High Street during one of the many fund raising weeks held throughout the conflict. Leading the contingent is Ernest Marchant, a solicitor who went on to head the leading North Bucks legal firm of Ernest Marchant and Sons. The company had major offices in Bletchley and Olney.

was 25 years-old and working on a fruit farm in Canada when war was declared in 1939. He returned to England as quickly as he could to help out on his uncle Fred Fryer's farm, Hayfield Farm in Aspley Guise, accessible via the railway crossing at the end of Berry Lane, off Salford Road.

The farm was typical of many country holdings at that time, growing a whole range of crops as well as having a sizeable dairy herd, the milk being sold direct to the householder via the traditional village milk round or to other roundsmen for

their use. Indeed, on the Friday lunchtime in 1940 that Aspley was bombed, Jim Broadbent was sitting at the farm making up the milk round book when he heard the explosions and the table on which he was working bounced up and down. What he didn't know was that he would go home to Bedford Road to find a hole in his roof! The Home Guard unit met in The Bell yard on Wednesday evenings and Sunday mornings under the command of Captain Bob Sims, the landlord of the pub. The unit sergeant was Tom Butcher, one of

Jim Broadbent, the last surviving member of the Aspley Guise Home Guard, pictured in August 2000 at the door of his home in Bedford Road. The house was damaged in the 1940 bombing.

the two village postmen, and he lived in Spinney Lane.

Jim recalls the Sunday morning .22 practice in the sand pit in Mill Lane, which later became the home of a small tank repair unit, the workshop hidden under the surrounding trees and by camouflaged 'scrim' netting. Later, he tells me, they were able to practise with the standard .303 Lee Enfield rifle at a full-sized firing range at Marston Moretaine, about half a dozen miles away on the Bedford road.

One of the worst jobs they had to do was to guard the mouth of the railway tunnel at Ampthill, on the main St Pancras line, in case enemy agents, dropping by parachute, should use it as a rendezvous point. They went on duty at 7pm in the evening and finished at 7am next morning, then went straight off to work. They managed some sleep on these nights, for the actual guard duty was on a rota system with two hours on and four off.

The 2am-4am shift was the worst to draw, Jim remembers, because at about half-past two in the morning a coal train would come through, with a steam engine at both front and back. Guarding the tunnel meant standing very close to the track and the tunnel entrance itself, so when this train came along whoever was on duty got covered in smoke, soot and steam not from one engine, but two. It meant going home with face, hands and uniform blackened but following these guard duties they were always rewarded with a good cooked breakfast before they disbanded to start their normal day's work.

In Dad's Army vein, Jim remembers one night when they were sent to guard the petrol dump at Husborne Crawley, which I mentioned in Chapter 3.

It seems it was a really murky night which became worse as it began to drizzle, which then turned to soaking rain. The word was passed round that everything seemed quiet so the Home Guard retired to the on-site canteen for the evening, snug in the warm and dry. All except, that was, for the platoon's equivalent of Private Pike, who somehow never got the message to retire and spent the whole night outside, shivering in the rain and wondering where everyone else had got to!

The Bell pub, where the Home Guard met, is on the corner of School Lane, now Woburn Lane, where it meets The Square. On the other side is what is now an imposing modern restaurant and hotel known as Moore Place. Before and during the war, this was a large residence known as The Holt.

A group of Land Army girls outside The Holt form wheelbarrows for the benefit of the camera.

The Holt was put to a variety of uses during the years of conflict, being in turn used by the Army, the Government Code and Cypher school based at Bletchley Park, and, towards the end of the war, by the Land Army as a hostel for the land girls.

To join the Land Army a girl had to be 17 years-old and, once accepted, did three months training covering a variety of farming methods and various skills. One of the training camps for Bedfordshire was at Potton, on the Cambridge side of Bedford, with another at Toddington, towards Luton, and from

Threshing was an all the year round job where the Land Army girls travelled from farm to farm.

there the qualified girls, who were paid a couple of pounds a week but provided with accommodation and food, would be billeted out. Their normal billet was a hostel of some kind and rarely did they live on a particular farm, for their work moved them from place to place according to the time of the year and the tasks that needed doing.

Frances Guttridge was a Lewisham, London, girl who was just two months short of her thirteenth birthday when war was declared. Just over five years later, Frances found herself posted to The Holt in Aspley Guise, where, as a fully fledged land girl, she worked on a number of local farms, including Mr Summerford's farm at Salford where earlier Sam Beasley's family had rented the farmhouse. Francis remembers Mr Summerford as a man with huge hands who could carry twenty chickens' eggs at a time .

To get back to her home in London she used to hitch-hike from Aspley Guise via the A5 Watling Street because she couldn't afford the train fare. Later, the hitch-hiking stopped, for Frances met and married Bill Jones, a local man who was an excellent accordion player. For many years Frances has lived in the family home in Aspley Hill, Woburn Sands, though sadly Bill died some years ago.

Sylvia Bunnett - Bunny to her land girl friends - hailed from Edmonton, in north London, and managed to get into the Land Army six months earlier than the stipulated 17 years limit because she was with her elder sister, who had also joined.

Sylvia went through her three months training at Toddington before moving on to The Holt in 1945 where she met Frances for the first time. They became friends and Sylvia, like Frances, married a local man, Jim Cox, the brother of Charlie Cox, one of the Aspley Guise men killed in the war. When, after the war, houses were built in the fields between The Weathercock pub in Woburn Sands and the back end of Aspley golf course - the development we now know as Burrough's Close - Jim and Sylvia made it their home and are still there today.

Josie Walton began her Land Army career in Westoning, where her family lived. After working on a farm in the village she transferred to Ravensden, still in Bedfordshire, where she trained new girls joining the Land Army in dairy work.

Josie came to The Holt and while there worked at Hayfield Farm alongside Jim Broadbent. Just after the war, in February 1946, she was one of many Bedfordshire land girls who took part in an exhibition of their work and a rally at Shire Hall which was opened by Princess Elizabeth, now The Queen. In 1947 Josie left the Land Army to rejoin her family at their new home, The Royal Oak at Woburn, where her father, Ben, was publican. Ben went on to become a popular licensee in the area, later being landlord at The Weathercock in Woburn Sands. Josie, now Josie Rowe, lives in Vicarage Street, Woburn Sands.

Though the agricultural work undertaken by the girls was often physically demanding, they still found time for relaxation and fun and games. As well as the cinema at Bletchley there was a variety of entertainment on offer at the Parish Hall, only a stone's throw from The Holt.

It was here that they particularly enjoyed the Saturday evening dances, even though they were often accused by the village girls of only being there to steal the local boys!

The pranks and japes inside The Holt were numerous, particularly one 'ghost-catching' session. It seemed that several of the girls had woken up during the night to sense some sort

Still in uniform but relaxing at the end of the day. Land Army girls in the recreation room at The Holt.

of presence in the room with them and were convinced the place was haunted. In best St Trinians fashion they decided that a bucket of water balanced over a slightly open door would do the trick. When the 'ghost' came in, down would come the bucket and the spectre would get soaked. Or that was the theory, except it wasn't a ghost, but one of the land girls playing her own tricks and spreading the tales of the place being haunted. After the bucket came down and the 'ghost' caught - it turned out to be a young girl named Rosa who later married Bill Kirkup, an Aspley man and lived in Mount Pleasant next door to Dolly Deacon - the mysterious presence in the rooms was never felt again!

Wherever members of the armed forces were stationed during the war, so the Women's Voluntary Service - the WVS

All girls together! Members of the Land Army contingent billeted at The Holt enjoy a social evening towards the end of the war.

The WVS at Woburn Sands serve tea to members of 339 Company, The Pioneer Corps. Guin Parker is furthest from the camera of the four.

were on hand to bring a touch of home by means of providing canteen facilities. Organised on a county basis, the WVS of Aspley Guise came under one administrative area, whilst Woburn Sands and nearby Bow Brickhill fell under another, all three villages having at some time or another during the war soldiers camped out or billeted nearby. At Aspley Guise Eleanor Allen became the focal point for WVS activity, combining this task with her billeting officer duties and other work. In Woburn Sands, Mrs Roscoe was in charge and with her volunteers set up canteen facilities in the Ellen Pettit Memorial Hall, in the High Street, from where cups of tea, sandwiches, cakes and biscuits brought cheer to soldiers in the Pioneer Corps and their drivers who served with the Royal Army Service Corps.

One of Mrs Roscoe's volunteers was Guin Parker, the

daughter of Mr Arthur Parker, the Woburn Sands billeting officer. Guin, who was 16 years-old when the war started, recalls how the Woburn Sands WVS was roughly split into two groups, one doing the canteen work, of which she was a member, the other doing the wartime equivalent of recycling by collecting silver paper used to line cigarette packets, newspapers and all kinds of other materials that could be reused in some way to help the war effort. The collections were stored at the back of Mr Elliot's grocery shop in the High Street.

Mrs Roscoe lived in the first bungalow in Woodland Way, Woburn Sands which, later modified with the addition of an upper storey, is now the home of Mary Manning's daughter.

It was the Pioneer Corps' job to erect what at first glance appeared to be dome-shaped corrugated iron huts with no end walls. We soon learned that they were ammunition storage shelters but were unaware that this was part of the build up of supplies for the invasion of Normandy on 6 June 1944.

The shelters sprang up alongside the road and tracks not only in the local woods but throughout the area generally. I remember going on the bus to Bedford one day and seeing mile after mile of the shelters stretching from Ridgmont to Ampthill, though I doubt they would have been spotted by any German reconnaissance aircraft, for most were sited on the wide verges and under the canopy offered by the roadside trees.

In Bow Brickhill woods, over towards Longslade and where one of the golf courses is now sited, there was an army camp complete with its own small parade ground and its flagpole surrounded by white-washed stones. Nearly thirty years after the war I found some of the stones still in place while out

At Bow Brickhill the WVS served refreshments in the Church Hall. In this picture village infant school teacher Miss M. Farnsworth offers sandwiches while Mrs Lily Gilks, an aunt of the author's wife and shown on the far left of the group of ladies, offers more goodies. Miss Farmsworth lodged with the Gilks family for many years.

walking my dog. The Pioneers also had a hutted encampment on the site of what is now Parkway, in Bow Brickhill, and many older people in the village still refer to the site as the camp field.

The Bow Brickhill WVS operated from the Church Hall, in Church Road, next door to The Plough pub, run by Jack and Nellie Foulkes. Between the pub and the Church Hall the small strip of ground became the site of the cookhouse for the Pioneers in the camp field. The kindly army cooks always seemed to find a plate of roast meat for the gaggle of village children who congregated at the foot of the steps of the Church Hall when attracted by the cooking aromas.

The Church Hall was also used by the Bow Brickhill Home Guard under the command of William Garratt, who lived at Pine Cottage, at the top of Bow Brickhill's steep hill and close to All Saints church. And the Private Pike syndrome was also alive and well here, too, it seems.

Mr Garratt, later to be known in the village as 'Honey' Garratt when he began to keep bees, was giving a lecture on the defence of the village. One Home Guard member was not paying attention, the story goes, but was trying to sneak a quick puff of a Woodbine cigarette instead. Suddenly, Mr Garratt barked out: 'That man. What steps would you take if the enemy invaded Bow Brickhill?'

'Mighty great big 'uns!' came the reply.

CHAPTER 7

LOCAL PERSONALITIES

All village communities have their personalities and characters and Woburn Sands and Aspley Guise were no exception during those war years. They also have religion, which in times of stress, such as we then experienced, can be of great comfort.

Though most denominations were represented in the two communities, the four people I best remember associated with religion were Rev. John Shelton, the sixth vicar of St Michael's at Woburn Sands, and in Aspley Guise, the Rev. Harry Clothier, rector of St Botolph's, Pastor Charles Davis, of the Courtney Memorial Hall and Mrs Elsie Fowler of the Methodist Chapel in Mount Pleasant, the lady who gave Billy Blowes a home and was my piano teacher.

I remember Rev. Shelton visiting Aspley Heath school occasionally and even then, in 1940-41, he had been rector at St Michael's for almost thirty years, arriving in the village in 1913. I am reliably informed that in 1920, when the church was given a measure of self government by the setting up of the new Parochial Church Council, Mr Shelton was very much against it, for he regarded the move as reducing the powers of the vicar.

Rev. Shelton married twice, with five children from his first marriage, a son John, who was killed during the war, and four daughters. In 1930, at the age of 69, he married Jean Hetherington, a nursing sister working at Homewood convalescent home, almost next door to the church, and the next year became the father of twins, Anthony and Michael.

A man who cared deeply for his parishioners, he was extremely highly thought of and following a period of declining health in his later years, he died just after the war, in 1946, at the age of 85. His wife stayed on in Woburn Sands after his death and when the vicarage was demolished and the current accommodation for senior citizens built on its site and named after him - Shelton Court - Mrs Shelton became one of its residents. She died in 1985.

Another visitor to our Aspley Heath school was the internationally well-known Dr H.H. Mann, of Husborne Crawley, who was the chairman of the school managers. Keenly interested in the welfare of children, Dr Mann headed up the Husborne Crawley site of the Rothamsted Experimental Farm at Harpenden. He regularly welcomed parties of school children to the Crawley site, which was past The White Horse pub on the way to Ridgmont station, where he would tell them about his experimental work on clover, soya beans and maize. He died in 1961 at the age of 89.

Among the first adults I acquainted in Woburn Sands however, outside Mrs Medcalf, Mr and Mrs Circuitt and our immediate neighbours, was a man who as a postman in Woburn Sands was literally known to everyone. He was Mr Tom Garrett.

In those days postmen in the villages delivered their letters with the help of a push-bike, for the luxury of post vans was still a long way off. In all weathers they pedalled along the roads and lanes of the area delivering the mail, using their standard issue General Post Office (GPO) bike, a big, heavy framed job with a flat, tray-like rack on the front which held their bag of letters and small packages.

Tommy Garrett - though he was always Mr Garrett to us children - rode his with some aplomb, for his old briar pipe was always clenched firmly in his mouth, whilst at the same time he rendered a variety of tunes in a wavering sort of hum which became his particular trademark. Tommy married twice, his first wife being a victim of the Fenny Stratford disaster before the war when a bus on which she was travelling was in collision with a train at the Simpson Road crossing. At the end of his long career as the village postie, Tom left Woburn Sands to live in Wales and died some years ago. His daughter from his second marriage, now Mrs Priscilla Knight, lives in San Remo Road, Aspley Guise.

Bill Begley, the local sweep, lived in Wavendon and like Tom Garrett, used a bike to make his rounds. Bill would arrive very early in the morning - sometimes before 6am - with his sweep's brushes expertly balanced on his shoulder as he cycled along. No-one to my knowledge ever saw them fall off. He would rig up a sheet with a hole in the centre in front of the fireplace, then, one by one, the sweeping rods would be screwed together by their brass ferrules and disappear through the hole in the sheet to sweep the chimney thoroughly. How he never spread soot everywhere I will never know, but after he had swept the chimney and tidied the hearth, it was as clean as a new pin and you would never know he had been. His son, Frank, carried on the trade, still using a bike, and now lives at Bow Brickhill.

Mr Arthur W. Parker, the Woburn Sands billeting officer, came to the village from Essex in 1921 following service in the army. A Fellow of the Surveyors' Institute he worked with Mr Wallace A. Foll who ran a company specialising in land agency work and property management. Later, Mr Parker was to partner Mr Foll's son, John, in the firm of Foll and Parker.

Arthur Parker enjoying an evening out many years after the war.

Getting evacuees into comfortable homes was not Mr Parker's only wartime role; his job as a property management professional brought him into contact with people at Bletchley Park and he played a leading role in finding suitable, but discreet, accommodation for particular teams and individuals. He was also an air raid warden and fire watcher, the latter task shared with his daughter Guin and others when they slept, six to an overnight watch, in the Scout Hut in Sandy Lane. Mr Parker was an active Parish Councillor, being deputy chairman, and organised many of the Woburn Sands fund raising weeks for the war effort. He also served for many years on the Parochial Church Council and was recognised as a talented local historian.

In an earlier chapter I have mentioned Dr Brian Furber, who came to Woburn Sands in the late 1930s and set up practise. During the war Dr Furber served as an RAF officer in France and was stationed for some time at RAF Benson, in Oxfordshire, and at nearby Cranfield.

Though plagued by back trouble after he left the RAF at the end of the war, he became a long serving Parish Councillor alongside Arthur Parker, as well as continuing to be a popular GP. A stalwart of Aspley Guise cricket club it was here that he joined forces,

Stan Brown showing his care for members of the Aspley Guise community in the mid-1960s. In this picture he is at The Cedars, Ampthill, visiting my grandfather, Fred Enever, who died at this Beds County Council residence in 1967, aged 86. It was also at The Cedars where my mother passed away, in 1984, at the age of 75. My father died in 1982, also aged 75.

in cricketing terms at least, with perhaps one of the best known Aspley Guise men of his time, Stanley Brown.

Stan Brown was born and bred in the village, the son of a skilled boot and shoe maker whose trade sign above his front door also told that repairs were 'neatly executed.' Stan grew up here - the family home at 51 West Hill where his son, Bob, who was born in 1926, lives still - with a love of cricket, though it was a game he was destined never to play, suffering ill health in his formative years to such an extent that he was treated at St Thomas' hospital in London and told to keep away from all sport.

But that didn't stop Stan becoming involved in his favourite game and for some forty years, from the mid 1920s onward, he was secretary and scorer of the cricket club. And that was not his only contribution to village life.

At about the same time as he took on his cricket club duties, he became clerk to the Parish Council, a job he carried on throughout and long after the war. One of his tasks as war approached was to canvass the village in respect of issuing Identity Cards, and this he did with the help of a Mr George Wilsher, before handwriting the card details and then delivering them all personally.

As Parish Clerk he was responsible for all the Parish Hall bookings and during the war these included the Tuesday evening film shows organised by a well-liked and much respected man, the late Dick Sinfield. Dick's family were the village builders and he was very much a movie camera buff. He filmed many aspects of village life both during and after the war and much of this footage has been used on television, both by Anglia TV and BBC2 in its Home Movie series of 1985.

At these Tuesday showings Stan issued the tickets while his young son Bob acted as assistant projectionist to Dick. The films were also shown at Woburn on Monday evenings and Woburn Sands on Thursday, with the intrepid trio freely giving their time so that villagers might be entertained. The forthcoming films were advertised in the various villages, particularly in the Post Offices where, at Aspley Guise, Stan's sister-in-law, Miss Alice Holmes, was postmistress. Stan was also verger at St Botolph's church, Aspley Guise, for many years, working closely during the war with Rev. Harry Clothier, the rector.

THE CLUB IN 1931 CELEBRATED ITS DIAMOND JUBILEE AND GAVE A GREAT OPPORTUNITY TO THE GREY BEARDS TO TALK OF PAST PERFORMANCES AND LONG SERVICE FAMILIES.

THE BARNWELLS WOULD NATURALLY ARISE. TODAY, BERNARD BARNWELL, BOWLER, BATSMAN AND VICE—CAPTAIN, CARRIES ON THE FAMILY TRADITION.

MR H. STANLEY BROWN KEEPS THE RECORDS OF THE CLUB AS SECRETARY AND SCORER AND HIMSELF HOLDS WHAT MUST BE A RECORD, FOR HE HAS TOTALLED UP THE RUNS AND WICKETS FOR FORTY YEARS.

A.E.B.
1947

CRICKET WAS SUCH A FEATURE OF THE VILLAGE AT THE END OF THE LAST CENTURY THAT A CRICKET WEEK WAS AN ANNUAL EVEN

How the Woburn Reporter - the local newspaper at the time - saw Stan Brown's involvement with Aspley Guise Cricket Club. The Reporter was then part of the Beds Times Group whose main office was in Mill Street, Bedford. The district office for the Reporter was in Downham Road, Woburn Sands, with Jim Purcell the local news gatherer. Jim lived in Theydon Avenue.

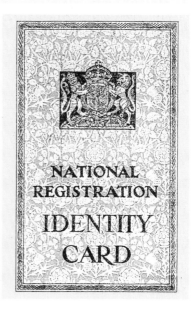

NATIONAL REGISTRATION IDENTITY CARD

The National Identity Card, issued to every member of the population. It was these that Stan Brown filled in by hand and then delivered personally.

114

Stan somehow managed to combine the busy life of wartime Parish Clerk and church warden with being an air raid warden as well, doing the rounds of the village regularly after dark to make sure that the strict blackout regulations were enforced. But as Parish Clerk he was part of the team responsible for fund raising weeks when money was collected for the war effort.

● Salute The Soldier Week in 1944. Aspley Guise overtakes its target of £8,000 and raises £11,325 for the war effort.

Aspley's efforts on fund raising in 1944 given coverage by the local press.

The weeks were given patriotic names such as 'War Weapons Week' and 'Salute the Soldier Week' and for the latter, in 1944, Aspley Guise comfortably exceeded its £8000 target by raising £11,325.

As I mentioned earlier, caring for the spiritual side of the village alongside Harry Clothier and others was Pastor Charles Davis. Pastor Davis and Rev. Clothier were not unfriendly, but seldom mixed in the same circles. This might have been because

Pastor Charles Davis, seated, front row, with his Courtney Memorial Hall congregation in 1944. Mrs Freda Maddy is seated, extreme left, front row. The building seen with the felt roof behind the hall was used as a social club by soldiers billeted locally.

Harry Clothier would never, within his services, pray for victory by force of arms. Yes, he would pray for the safety of our soldiers, but never for victory by the use of guns and bullets. And, by all accounts, he enjoyed a pint of Bob Sims beer now and then, especially after Sunday evening Evensong. Rev. Clothier, later Canon Clothier, moved from Aspley after the war to Sharnbrook, near Bedford, and later, I believe, went to live in Wales.

Pastor Davis - 'Chum' to his family and friends - came to Aspley Guise from Beckenham, in Kent, in the mid-1920s. He was ordained into the Baptist Church and before coming to Aspley often held services on the beach at the seaside resort of Ryde where he would have an altar made of pebbles. He came to Aspley to be Pastor of the Courtney Memorial Hall, in The Square, where Sunday services were regularly held.

His home was in The Manse, then one of the two houses built side-on to Bedford Road just past Mount Pleasant on the way to Husborne Crawley and now numbered 36. He was a keen sportsman, playing both golf and cricket within the village, and during the war often refereed soccer matches.

In the Courtney Memorial Hall he began 'Star Band' for the young people of the village, what we would today probably call a youth club, and it had the motto, 'Look Up and Aim High.' He was very well liked and was always happy to take people in his car to the doctors or dentists if they were under the weather or the time of their appointment didn't fit in with the bus or train timetables.

Pastor Davis left the village shortly after the war to live in St Leonard's Avenue, Bedford, close to the now defunct St John's railway station. He preached at St Mary's church in

Tom Povey with his sideshow at one of the many garden fetes held at the home of the Allen family. The lady on the extreme left is a Mrs Davis - no relation to the Pastor as far as she is aware - and the pair to the right of Tom Povey are my mother, partly hidden, and with the cigarette, my Aunt Vi.

Bedford before moving to Clapham where he taught religious education at the Silver Jubilee schools. His final ministry was at Alfreton, in Sussex where, getting ready to take a service in the early 1960s, he complained of feeling unwell, collapsed and died. He was close to 80 years-old.

Mary Manning's father, Tom Povey, was much more than the local water board engineer. A keen musician - he played saxophone - he and his band often provided music for the many dances held at the Parish Hall and he could always be relied upon to run a stall at the village fete.

Being an engineer, Tom did not find it difficult to devise a sideshow whereby a model aeroplane whirled over a circular board divided into segments, each segment being home to a prize of varying value. When the electric current was cut off, the plane slowly came to a halt, and if it stopped over your segment, you picked up the prize. We kids found it fascinating, but better still was to cadge a ride in Mr Povey's car, a big black Rover that we all admired. Tom retired as the water board engineer in 1965.

Tommy Garrett's postmen counterparts in Aspley Guise were Tom Butcher, the sergeant in the Home Guard platoon, and Albert Munn, and, along with the various shopkeepers and traders, they were part of our everyday life as children. At that time Aspley boasted a variety of small shops and businesses, most in or near The Square. Mrs Whitmore's 'Little Shop' was at the bottom of West Hill, opposite Dr Richardson's surgery,

Aspley Guise Post Office, run by Miss Alice Holmes, in the 1930s. Albert Munn is the postman by the phone box, which was later moved to the church side of The Anchor pub's entrance. Later it was moved to its present position, the other side of the entrance nearest The Square.

selling sweets, ice cream and all kinds of household items. When it came to garden fetes, Mrs Whitmore proved the true entrepreneur, loading ice creams into a cold box and getting them delivered to the fete's location by the owner of the village taxi firm, Mr Teddy Sibley, who operated from premises very close to Pastor Davis' Manse in Bedford Road.

In The Square proper was Miss Holmes' Post Office, Fred Maynard's boot and shoe repair business, Thompson's the barber's, Watson's the bakers, a greengrocery-cum-general store run by Miss Hodges, Mr Tripp's newsagent and tobacconist and the major grocery shop, run in the 1930s by a Mr Porter, who eventually sold out to the Dudeney and Johnston chain.

Tom Crute had a grocery and provisions shop next to Watson's the bakers and proved to be a very lucky man, winning outright a few years before the war, the Irish Sweepstake. With his massive fortune - in those days, at least - of some £30,000, he retired, and by the beginning of the war was living in some splendour in a large, detached house built at the junction of Gypsy Lane and Mount Pleasant. He and his wife, accompanied by a relative, a Miss or Mrs Higgins - I confess as a youngster I was never sure which - would be seen most Sunday evenings on their way to the Mount Pleasant chapel with the ladies wearing the most opulent dresses of velvet or silk and looking very grand indeed.

At the Woburn Sands end of the village the Duke's Head pub, on the corner of Duke Street, was still a going concern while at the other end, in Mount Pleasant, the Barnwell family ran its very successful butcher's business.

Between my home and the Barnwell shop premises, which

were opposite The Wheatsheaf, was Mr Hunt's shop on the corner of San Remo Road. Micky Hunt was from the fictional Arkwright school of traders, made famous by Ronnie Barker in the TV series 'Open All Hours,' I reckon, for he would sell you anything. I recall going in to his shop one day to ask if he had any sweets, which he hadn't, but still coming out wondering why I had bought a packet of Rennie's indigestion tablets! Well, they looked a bit like sweets, I suppose.

Then there were the milkmen; Rupert Alley, who delivered bottled milk but always had a small churn of fresh milk on hand in case he sold out of bottles, and who never forgot to touch his cap in greeting or farewell to any of his customers. And both Mr Brown - 'Milky' Brown - a small, slim man who quite accepted his nickname and who lived to a ripe old age in a council house almost opposite the Mount Pleasant chapel, and Harry Young from West Hill. There were all sorts of other door to door deliveries, too, in those days, for there were mobile butcheries and greengrocers, Mr Tansley and others made deliveries of paraffin oil, the bakers brought bread every day or at worst every other day, and the coalman, the job my father did for a time, was still a familiar sight, hawking bags of coal from door to door. It was all a world away from the one stop supermarket we know today. But it was a world where you could leave the milk, or bread or coal money on the front step and know that the only person who would take it would be the rightful trader.

Woburn Sands always boasted the bigger variety of shops and in The Square, nearest to Aspley Heath school, was Mrs Richardson's sweets and general goods shop. On the corner of Aspley Heath was another shop which at some stage during

A military band leads a parade through the High Street, Woburn Sands, where part of the wide range of shops can be clearly seen. In the top left of the picture the War Memorial on its old site is just visible.

the war, I believe, was taken over by Mr and Mrs Deacon - no relation to Malcolm as far as I know - and next to that, on the corner of Hardwick Road, was Partridge, the baker. On one side of The Square was The Swan pub, now a Beefeater restaurant, while on the other side was Leigh-Lancaster's shop and yard where the picture buses were garaged.

There was a range of shops running all the way down the east side of the High Street, much as they do today, with Mr Elliot's grocery shop to the fore, as was the Co-op grocery department, Emms jewellers next to what was then Tansley's second garage, the Post Office, George Wesley's hairdressing salon, begun, so he would often tell, when he had only half-a-crown (12p) to his name, and Mr White's fruit and veg shop

The Fire Brigade detachment, headed by the women members who played an important role in the wartime task, parade alongside the armed services and Home Guard contingents in a fund raising week.

where I remember queuing with my mother for a pound of tomatoes, the rationed amount Mr White allowed you to buy when his crop from the Spring Grove greenhouses was ready. The two banks, Westminster and Barclays, were in the same position as they are today, there was Bill Shortland's shoe repair workshop, Miss Amy Wagstaff's shoe shop and more trading premises, including Wooding's wet fish shop, going all the way down to the corner of Russell Street which boasted an ironmonger's, as it still does to this day.

Within this last run of shops, sitting a few doors down from the Westminster Bank, was W.H. Smith & Sons, the newsagents, stationers and booksellers. It was a well patronised shop, much loved by us kids if only for the wonderful array of pencils, both coloured and ordinary, rulers, rubbers and other materials that we could use at school. And there were pencil cases.

I pestered my parents to buy me one while we still lived in Woburn Sands but they professed never to be able to find the

A Woburn Sands fund raising parade concludes in the Recreation Ground.

shop! It seems my interpretation of local speech as told by my school chums, then translated into my cockney accent, led me to tell my parents that you could buy pencil cases at 'Smivensens' and I think they must have walked the High Street a dozen times before they managed to work it out. I know that my Dad and the shop manager had a good laugh over it while I just cringed with embarrassment.

There were other shop premises scattered around the village. On the corner of The Grove, opposite the recreation ground and where my uncle and aunt and grandparents went to live, was another general store, while closer to Weathercock Lane was the Station Stores, now an interior designers, and another shop. There was a small shop in The Leys, close to the junction with Bow Brickhill road and a collection of shops nestling at the foot of Aspley Hill, close to The Square. One of these was a shop selling dress and curtain materials called Rowlands Fabrics while on the other side of the road was another favourite shop, Deeley's, a bakery, which sold the most wonderful cakes you could imagine when Lou Deeley, the proprietor, could get hold of the right ingredients. Lou, or Mr Deeley as of course children needed to call him, was a wonderful character with a wicked sense of humour, a trait inherited by his son, Tony, who became a friend of mine some years later.

CHAPTER 8

TOWARDS VICTORY AND CHANGE

As 1943 progressed there was positive proof that the tide of war was changing in favour of the Allies. In May, Axis forces in North Africa surrendered, leaving the way clear for our landings on Sicily some two months later, and in just over a month the island was cleared of opposition. Italian leader Mussolini was overthrown and arrested and Italy changed sides in October and declared war on Germany. By this time Allied forces were already on the offensive on the Italian mainland.

On other fronts the Russians had stemmed the German advances and were now retaking large chunks of their homeland while in the Pacific, United States, British, Australian and other British Empire troops were beginning to dislodge the Japanese.

We children followed the news avidly on the wireless and pored over the maps that appeared almost every day in the newspapers, detailing the scale of Allied advances. But I think there were two other things that were probably more important to us youngsters at the time; double summer time, so it didn't get dark until eleven at night, and the arrival of American troops, mainly in the form of support units to the American Eighth Airforce.

The American Airforce set up bomber bases throughout

126

East Anglia with the nearest to us at Aspley probably being those on the far side of Bedford. Thurleigh immediately springs to mind although there were American personnel at Cardington and at Chicksands, near Shefford, as well. All of us, young and old alike, could not help but admire the smartness of their uniforms compared to our men's regulation issue and I remember thinking that they all looked so fit and well fed. When we kids discovered that ice cream was a regular part of their diet at their camps and bases, we resolved to make as many friends as we could!

For their part the Americans liked the charm of our village pubs, though not what they referred to as the 'warm' beer, and with a large percentage of the local men away in the armed forces, some of the local girls found them willing escorts. It wasn't long before the classic phrase 'over sexed, over paid and over here' was being coined by their detractors, for it was certainly true that as well as having the pick of the girls they always seemed to have plenty of cash. Not that such problems worried us youngsters, who were more keen on accepting their gifts of chocolate and sweets - or 'candy' as we learned they called them - and the Amercian standby, chewing gum. I remember one of the first phrases of greeting we used on meeting them initially was: 'Got any gum, chum?'

The Americans were always around in the pubs during the evenings because of the bombing strategies then in operation by them and the RAF. The RAF bombed German targets at night, the Americans bombed during the day.

This meant that we on the ground could watch their massive formations of Flying Fortress aircraft streaming towards their targets around breakfast time, see them come back in the late afternoon, then see the British Lancasters going out later that evening. When the Lancasters came back in the early morning we were still asleep.

Sometimes we children would try and count how many American planes went out in the morning and compare them with the number that came back, but of course that didn't give a true picture of losses, for planes might make emergency landings elsewhere. What we did see though, was the number of Fortresses which came back bearing the scars of both anti-aircraft fire and fierce combat against the German fighters. How some of the planes stayed in the air I don't know, for they would come back with holes in their wings, one or sometimes even two of the four engines stopped, chunks missing from the high tailplane and bits chewed out of the fuselage. The damage was a regular talking point among us boys as we compared what we had seen, usually preceding a game of 'Aircraft' which was a favourite.

One of us would stand three paces in front of however many were in the playing group and shout out the initials of an aircraft - HH for Hawker Hurricane, or BPD for Boulton Paul Defiant, for example. Whoever guessed it would then have to reach forward to touch the caller, and so take over themselves as caller. If none of the group could come up with he right answer, the caller could begin to spell out the name, but for each letter given, moved another pace away. If this happened and finally it was guessed, there were all manner of contortions put to the test in an effort to reach out and touch the caller!

Now deep into the fourth year of war we had all begun to take rationing and the general austerity as part of everyday life. I wore boots now like the rest of the boys but mother still wouldn't budge on the balaclava issue! As the winter came on, though, she produced a brown corduroy zip-up lumber jacket, which I recall I almost lived in, but which was tough, serviceable, warm and very comfortable, especially as by now I had my own bike. This meant I was no longer dependent on the bus to get to school and could get home quicker in the afternoon, so allowing more time for all those wonderful schoolboys activities of rabbiting, scrumping apples, or playing cricket or football, depending on the time of year.

I think it must have been that winter, 1943-44, that we had some very severe frosts that left wonderful patterns in the ice that froze inside my bedroom window. The Walsh boys, Alan Ball, Malcolm Deacon, myself and others trekked off to a series of rectangular ponds, known as the canals, which we reached by cutting through a copse of trees and brushwood on one side of The Close. I still don't know who owned them then, or if they are still in existence today, but certainly they were a magnet for young and old alike when they froze over during those wartime winters.

Swapping ordinary boots for wellingtons we boys would cut out a slide on one side of a particular pond or else begin an impromptu game of ice hockey, finding a suitable stick in a hedge or, if forethought was the order of the day, taking one with us. The puck was any bit of stone or wood, or perhaps more realistically, a large pencil rubber. And how we envied those well-to-do adults who actually appeared with real ice skates!

Much nearer to home, San Remo Road became our toboggan run when enough snow fell. Having a very steep incline and not being made up, San Remo never received the

San Remo Road, Aspley Guise, a picture believed taken in 1916. It was this unmade surface that we used as our toboggan run. The road was given a proper surface in 1966 when housing was extended to where the sheds are pictured. The sheds went before the war and it was this area where cricket and rounders were played by the children in the 1940s and '50s. Mr Brown's orchard then occupied what is shown as ploughed land in front of the trees.

sprinkling of sand and grit from carters like Wyn Cook, who treated the roads in bad weather from their horses and carts, spreading the mixture by hand with a shovel. The result was that anything that would slide was pressed into service as a sledge, especially old metal tea trays, providing they were large enough to sit on. Some of the kids had proper shop bought toboggans that were the envy of us all, others had home made jobs that performed just as adequately.

I remember trying to concoct something half decent out of bits of wood and, for the runners, bits of iron hoop off an old and unused barrel, but carpentry was never my strong point and if it did stay together then it weighed a ton and seemed to stick in the snow instead of gliding over it. So, nine times out of ten, it was back to the tea tray, and you started your run in Turney's gateway, came across the road (Mount Pleasant) then leapt on your conveyance as soon as you could. With any luck an average run would take you down to where the road levelled out, a good one would get you as far as Polly Walsh's, and something really exceptional would take you as far as Mr Brown's orchard gates. Invariably though, the fun would come to an end as the San Remo householders decided that stepping out of their side entrances on to a sheet of ice was no joke. So down would go the hot ashes from the kitchen and living room fires and our toboggan run would be ruined. But then there was always Bumpstead.

Bumpstead was a field opposite the junction of West Hill and Wood Lane. It had a good steep slope but ended abruptly in a very steep bank that dropped down to the roadway. A flimsy fence of posts and barbed wire was all that stopped would-be champions on their sledges from ending up on the road in West Hill, though I believe that fate befell more than one Aspley youngster. Bumpstead as we knew it no longer exists; the houses built on what is now The Mount swallowed it up in the early 1960s. Sometimes we would be very brave and go even further afield to try out the classic Woburn Sands sledge runs at Tidbury, the top field that stretches away from Woodland Way, off The Leys, up towards Aspley Heath. But in truth that was a last resort, for getting there took time and that time could be put to other uses when there was snow on the ground - like the Mount Pleasant kids taking on those who lived around The Square in a snowball fight.

Les Page recalls one of those occasions very well. Tucked into the hedge that formed the San Remo frontage of Micky

Hunt's shop, he was lobbing snowballs up and over the hedge at those of us in Mount Pleasant and positioned outside Turneys' Mount Pleasant House and the cottages that ran back down the road towards Bedford Road. There was a lull in the proceedings as 'Bobby' Banks came by, but Les didn't know that, tucked into the hedge. The next thing he knew was being confronted by an irate policeman, helmet askew and covered in snow!

'Bobby' Banks and Les seemed to be inextricably drawn together, for the snowball incident was not the only time they clashed. Once, on the Bedford Road outside his home, Les rigged up a booby trap for John Jackson, Jim Broadbent's stepson, who lived opposite. It was a piece of string, stretched across the road and designed to catch John as he rode by on his bike. But it wasn't John who rode by......

My only direct experience with our erstwhile policeman came at about this time, 1943-44. It must have been late summer or autumn because the apples in Wyn Cook's little orchard opposite our cottage proved more and more tempting. One day I could resist it no longer.

One of my father's favourite dishes was apple pie and I thought that with him now serving in Italy, it might be nice if Mum made one so that we remembered him. And the apples were not ten yards from the front door, with only that prickly holly hedge keeping me at bay. Well, I went for it, scrumped the apples, and carried them back held in a pocket made by pulling up the front of my pullover. I was so intent on getting back safely through that prickly hedge that I didn't even see Mr Banks until I literally stumbled out of the hedge to find him waiting for me.

Now in those days children held the police in much more awe than do youngsters today. They really were the bastions of law and order in our society and if a policeman caught you at something you knew you faced two lots of trouble. One from the police, one from your parents when they were told.

I felt very frightened as Mr Banks asked me what I thought I was up to and what had I got in my pullover. He took the apples from me, leaving me very close to tears I recall, particularly when he said the dreaded words: 'I shall come and see your Mum later.' All my good intentions, it seemed, had gone totally wrong, though I was not to know all was not lost. It seems that Mr Banks first had a quick word with Wyn Cook, who took the view that boys will be boys and the loss of half-a-dozen or so cooking apples was forgivable in the

Garden fetes were organised by a variety of local organisations and brought the whole community together socially. A highlight was always the children's fancy dress parade, which usually began the proceedings. These young hopefuls are pictured at a fete on Aspley Common.

circumstances, then with my mother. Something along the lines of 'Don't let me catch him again, Dolly; now we'll share the apples between us!' was said, and we eventually had the apple pie so that we felt closer to Dad.

When the early months of 1944 came and went there was a marked increase in troop movements throughout the area. Convoys of lorries streamed through the village at all hours and now and then armoured vehicles, including heavy tanks, would take the same route. On the railway, trains loaded with British or American troops came from the Cambridge direction going west and goods trains loaded with guns, lorries, jeeps and other vehicles became a familiar site. One of the pastimes then was to go down to Aspley crossing, in Salford Road, and put a penny or a halfpenny on the rails to let the waggons pass over it. The end result was a flattened coin and we would compare whose coin ended up the thinnest. More than one, I know, ended up being drilled with a hole and turned into a souvenir necklace, especially if it was a newly minted coin which showed the current date.

The invasion of mainland France by Allied troops on 6 June 1944, or D-Day as it was to be known, told us why there had been so much military activity in the previous months. Now there were maps of new areas to be pored over in the newspapers as we eagerly followed the landings, breakouts from the beachheads, and subsequent advances and gains made by our forces. But at home, life for us children followed much the same pattern as it had done in previous years.

The Spring months meant football and birdnesting, and with the latter I could now tell by the shape and composition of a nest which bird was the occupant. This would be merely

With the cricket pavilion and mower shed in the background, youngsters queue for a pony ride at one of the Aspley Guise fetes.

Home on leave but still a job to do! A serving member of the Royal Navy gives the civvies a hand in an Aspley tug o' war contest.

confirmed by the size and colour of the eggs when they came along - the sky blue eggs of the hedge-sparrow, the speckled reddy-pink ones of the robin, the blue with black spots of the song thrush, and the sea green with brownish markings of the blackbird. I could tell the difference between swallows and house martins when they arrived from Africa in the early summer, listened avidly for the sound of the first cuckoo and searched high and low for a nest where this bird had laid its egg and where its chick would be reared by unsuspecting foster parents. A gang of us found only one, as I recall, during all those wartime years. It was in Gypsy Lane and the cuckoo had laid its egg in the nest of a hedge-sparrow. But we never got to see the young cuckoo reared; word got around as to the location of the nest site and somebody took the egg.

Even bird-nesting, though, had its practical side. Finding a pheasant or partridge nest meant supplementing the food ration, for these eggs made good eating and were preferable to dried egg if hens' eggs were hard to get. Wild duck and moorhens' eggs, too, were much prized if you could find them, with moorhens the easier of the two to come by. This we did by returning quietly to the canals, pinpointing the nests among the reeds and getting at the eggs with a simple but ingenious device. The nests, of course, were surrounded by water which was too deep to wade into. But by using a table spoon lashed to a long bamboo cane, you could reach out into the nest, slide the spoon under an egg, and carefully bring it to safety.

Summer meant fishing in the clay pit at Woburn Sands or at Salford Mill, and cricket or rounders at the bottom of San Remo, where the girls often joined in. Then there was fruit picking at the Ridgmont fruit farm, if you were lucky enough to get one of these sought after holiday jobs, and long, warm days spent splashing around in Crawley Brook where we would dam up the flow of water to create a pool sometimes four feet deep. We would all have the time of our lives splashing around in the none-too-clean water but then, when the weather cooled, there would be the awesome sight of the water rushing away as we destroyed our dam. Mind you, it was sometimes done for us if an irate farmer with land further downstream suddenly realised his cattle were going short of a drink.

The cornfields continued to be a great summer attraction when the crop was cut, for there was then always the chance of catching a rabbit. Poor Mr Bunny's hiding place became

Fetes were sometimes held at Radlett House, found between Weathercock Lane and West Hill and later offices of the Independent Counselling and Advisory Service (ICAS). For many years, including those of the war, Radlett House was a residential home for children, many of whom attended local schools. In this 1940s picture, Radlett House children play host to the local community and nearest the camera, left, is Pastor Davis' niece, Betty Saunders, later to become Betty Hulance. Betty and her husband Geoff, a well-known local plumber, live in Salford Road.

smaller and smaller as the field was harvested and by the final cut rabbits were often running everywhere. Chased by a yelling mob of motley children and adults it must have been very frightening for them and something I would discourage anyone from doing now. But then food was food and getting a rabbit stew or pie merely for the want of a chase was totally acceptable. Now and then the farmer, one of his men or some other adult would appear at the edge of the field with a shotgun and if a rabbit outran the chasing pack, it faced this new threat. Mr Crute, he of the Irish Sweepstake win, would sometimes appear in this way, armed with a little 410 shotgun. I never saw him hit anything, though.

By now the combine harvester was beginning to make an appearance but us kids didn't appreciate its work, for the stubble it left was much longer than that left by the old binder pulled by a tractor. The outcome of this was that for boys in short trousers, as we all were then, the combine stubble came at exactly shin height. Socks were invariably down round the ankles so the stubble pricked your shins like so many needles and at the end of the day your legs were red raw and very sore indeed.

By this phase of the war agricultural production was at its height and children over a certain age were allowed time off from school to help with the potato harvest. I didn't fall into this category but I did manage to get a Saturday job picking potatoes at Mr Orlebar's farm at Husborne Crawley. The field I worked in was known as The Park and was the first field past the last houses in Bedford Road, Aspley Guise. The particular field I remembered because, in my first summer in Aspley - 1942 - I had seen a gymkhana there, something I had never seen before, and I envied all the country youngsters with their ponies and horses as they competed in the various events.

It was certainly different seeing it as a potato field. I worked alongside adults that I knew, land girls and former Italian prisoners of war. A tractor with a 'spinner' attached to the back travelled up and down the rows of potatoes and the potatoes were dug and spun out of the ground. We pickers followed on, armed with buckets, and loaded the buckets with potatoes before taking them to sacks or other containers and tipping them over. It was hard and dusty work but it did mean a few shillings pocket money. Even though there were no sweets to buy it paid for a trip to the cinema via the picture bus or train. And my Mum saw some free potatoes.

We also earned money by doing odd jobs and the Miss, or Mrs Higgins - I got round it by using local dialect and calling her 'Mizz' which could have meant either - gave me and Malcolm Deacon the job one Saturday morning of clearing a load of ivy from around and on top of an old garden shed. Malc and I set to work with a will and soon had the sides cleared. Then we scrambled up on to the roof, each of us working from a separate end. What I didn't know was I had the end where the corrugated iron was rusted through and next minute I had hit the ground six feet below and was staring up at Malc peering down at me and asking was I alright! 'Mizz' Higgins heard the commotion, came hurrying out to see what was happening and the task was promptly put on hold while I was taken in to her beautifully furnished house and my cuts and bruises bathed. A cooling glass of lemonade and a slice of plain cake followed, plus the coppers for doing the job, so all in all and accident considered, it wasn't such a bad day.

It must have been about this time, the late summer of 1944, that my mother decided that we should spend a weekend with her father and stepmother who had stayed on in Canning Town throughout the war. There had been few air raids to speak off and mother obviously thought there was little risk involved.

Off we went and I enjoyed the journey and seeing things I hadn't seen for several years, even though there was still a vast amount of bomb damage. But I didn't like the noise and the general clamour of London and I felt hemmed in. On the Saturday evening the siren sounded and we made our way into Grandfather's Anderson shelter as the V1 flying bombs began to come over. I confess I felt a little queasy going down the steps into an Anderson again, and remembered that terrible night of 1940. But Gramp put me at ease and after a while had me back outside actually watching the doodle-bugs, as Londoners called the flying bombs, scudding across the sky. There was no danger while their motor was running, Gramp told me, but when it cut out, and if it was close by, then that's when you needed to dive for cover. As luck had it, none fell near that night.

Before we left to return to Aspley, I remember my Nan telling me that I was beginning to sound like a country boy when I spoke. I certainly had never given it a thought but it was true that my harsh London vowels were beginning to slip into the dipthonged sounds of the Beds-Bucks borders.

Once returned from the weekend, things continued their daily round in Aspley with our ball games in the streets and our foraging around the fields. I was still learning more and more about the country way of life and was able to identify all the different tree types that grew locally, something that perhaps grew out of necessity when finding oak trees from which we children collected acorns for pig food, as was mentioned in Chapter 5. By now I also knew why the leaves of the trees changed to those wonderful colours in autumn and how the sap stopped flowing to form a cork-like seal between leaf and twig so that eventually the leaf dropped off.

From neighbours working the allotments I began to pick up the rudiments of fruit growing and the different way top fruit - apples, plums and pears - needed to be cultivated and pruned, depending on whether the tree was being grown as a bush, fan, espalier or cordon. I learned about soft fruit too - plenty of woodash, for it contains potash, around gooseberries, plenty of manure for gross feeding blackcurrants.

I admired the delphiniums grown there by Mrs Freda Maddy, who was housekeeper at The Rookery in Salford Road where her husband, Alf, was the gardener. The house was the wartime home of Sefton Delmer, who headed a special intelligence unit which, by the end of the war, was operating from Milton Bryan. Others showed me how to plant leeks - make a hole a few inches deep with a dibber, just drop the leek plant in and water it well, allowing the water to wash the soil around the roots - and drummed in to me that all the cabbage family must be grown in firm ground. Cauliflowers, I was told, must really be grown without any check to their development and never sow carrots in freshly manured ground - it will fork the roots.

So autumn came with talk of the war being over by Christmas. But when Christmas came the Germans mounted a counter offensive in the Ardennes and by looking at those newspaper maps again, we knew there was still some way to go.

However, by February of 1945 it was clear that victory was now in sight, even if some of us children had other things on our minds in the shape of a trip to Bedford. Mrs Michael, our class teacher at Aspley Heath school, took a dozen or so of us off one day to a Bedford school where we sat a series of educational tests. It transpired it was the eleven plus exam and how well we performed would determine what level and pattern of education we were to follow in the coming years.

As March drifted into April we knew it was now only a matter of weeks before Germany was overthrown. The Russians in the east and the American and British armies in the west seemed to be in a race to capture Berlin and, as history tells us, it was the Russians who won. However, I remember those last few days of war as the time when I enjoyed my first banana for five or more years.

With foodstuff getting through because we had gained the upper hand over the U-boats, a consignment of bananas reached our shores. They were rationed, of course, and only available to those producing a child's green ration book. My younger cousin, Bob, just fell into this category so Aunt Vi queued for her allotted amount at Mr White's. Mother and I must have visited her in The Grove at Woburn Sands about the time because as we left to walk home, she gave me a banana. I didn't eat it; I sucked it like a lollipop, relishing its flavour after all those years, and made it last all the way to Aspley Square!

Then the European war was over. Prime Minister Winston Churchill announced that with Germany defeated we would celebrate with a Victory in Europe Day (VE-Day) on 8 May. There were street parties in every town and village in the country, church bells rang out - this was forbidden during the war as they were only to be used as a signal that we had been invaded - and everywhere you looked people were celebrating

VE-Day came in May 1945 and street parties were held everywhere. This shows Aspley Guise' Duke Street community at the celebrations.

Music for the Duke Street party came from Rupert Tyers on piano, Tom Povey, saxophone, and Bill Jones, accordion.

in one way or another. It was a truly wonderful time, but there was still the question of the war in the Pacific, where Japan was fighting on. But that came to an abrupt end in August, when the world entered the atomic era. Two atomic bombs, on

Hiroshima and Nagasaki, finally broke Japan's resolve. Now it was time for Victory over Japan Day (VJ-Day) and six years of global hostilities were at an end.

There were more celebrations, though for many of us children, now eleven years old, they marked not just the end of a

The world's first atomic mushroom billows upwards over Japan's Hiroshima on 6th August 1945. Three days later Nagasaki suffered the same fate. The world had entered a new scientific era.

A picture of the revellers at a Grand Dance at Aspley Guise Parish Hall, believed to be part of the VE celebrations.

terrible conflict but the end of a way of life. We had all mixed together as growing youngsters, enjoying the freedom of the countryside where community spirit was ever present and the society in which we lived largely free of both unemployment and crime, unlike today. Now things were to change as we began to go our separate ways: the eleven plus results sent me and others to school in Bedford, other classmates at Aspley Heath moved on to schools at Wolverton, some saw out their education still under Mr Codd's headship and the dedication of Mr Cooper and the senior girls' teacher, Miss Wells, later to become Mr Codd's second wife.

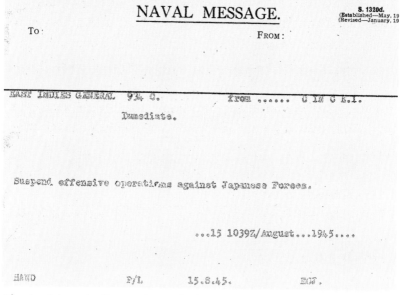

The signal from the Commander-in-Chief, East Indies, that curtailed the horrors of war. All hostilities ceased and six years of global conflict were at an end.

When a General Election was called the country turned its back on Winston Churchill, the leader of the wartime coalition government, and brought the Labour Party to power under

Clement Attlee, who had worked closely with Churchill in the wartime cabinet. The Labour Party proposed sweeping changes to society, not least the setting up of a National Health Service, which came into being in 1948, and the nationalisation of the utility industries and railways, among others.

And so the changes began, changes which all societies experience and live with, some for better, some for worse. Certainly today we are all richer in material possessions such as cars, fridges, freezers, telephones and televisions, things which all those years ago were only the province of the very wealthy. But we have lost out, I believe, in the ability to care about each other in the way we did during those war years. As villages and towns continue to expand and populations become more mobile, community spirit seems to be slipping away.

But all that, as they say, is another story. When the war began in September 1939 I was a typical inner city child; a year later I found myself within a rural environment. I loved it and its people and stayed on to make it my permanent home. The London accent went years ago, I married a Bow Brickhill girl, we made our home in that village and our two children, Mark and Rachel, were born there.

I came to such rural surroundings a true cockney kid. Now, when I look in the mirror some sixty years on, I like to think I see the face of a countryman.

Books Published by THE BOOK CASTLE

CHANGES IN OUR LANDSCAPE: Aspects of Bedfordshire, Buckinghamshire and the Chilterns 1947-1992: Eric Meadows. Over 350 photographs from the author's collection spanning nearly 50 years.

COUNTRYSIDE CYCLING IN BEDFORDSHIRE, BUCKINGHAMSHIRE AND HERTFORDSHIRE: Mick Payne. Twenty rides on and off-road for all the family.

PUB WALKS FROM COUNTRY STATIONS: Bedfordshire and Hertfordshire: Clive Higgs. Fourteen circular country rambles, each starting and finishing at a railway station and incorporating a pub stop at a mid way point.

PUB WALKS FROM COUNTRY STATIONS: Buckinghamshire and Oxfordshire: Clive Higgs. Circular rambles incorporating pub-stops.

LOCAL WALKS: South Bedfordshire and North Chilterns: Vaughan Basham. Twenty-seven thematic circular walks.

LOCAL WALKS: North and Mid Bedfordshire: Vaughan Basham. Twenty-five thematic circular walks.

FAMILY WALKS: Chilterns South: Nick Moon. Thirty 3 to 5 mile circular walks.

FAMILY WALKS: Chilterns North: Nick Moon. Thirty shorter circular walks.

CHILTERN WALKS: Hertfordshire, Bedfordshire and North Bucks: Nick Moon.

CHILTERN WALKS: Buckinghamshire: Nick Moon.

CHILTERN WALKS: Oxfordshire and West Buckinghamshire: Nick Moon. A trilogy of circular walks, in association with the Chiltern Society. Each volume contains 30 circular walks.

OXFORDSHIRE WALKS: Oxford, the Cotswolds and the Cherwell Valley: Nick Moon.

OXFORDSHIRE WALKS: Oxford, the Downs and the Thames Valley: Nick Moon. Two volumes that complement Chiltern Walks: Oxfordshire, and complete coverage of the county, in association with the Oxford Fieldpaths Society. Thirty circular walks in each.

THE D'ARCY DALTON WAY: Nick Moon. Long-distance footpath across the Oxfordshire Cotswolds and Thames Valley, with various circular walk suggestions.

THE CHILTERN WAY: Nick Moon. A guide to the new 133 mile circular Long-Distance Path through Bedfordshire, Buckinghamshire, Hertfordshire and Oxfordshire, as planned by the Chiltern Society.

JOURNEYS INTO BEDFORDSHIRE: Anthony Mackay. Foreword by The Marquess of Tavistock, Woburn Abbey. A lavish book of over 150 evocative ink drawings.

JOURNEYS INTO BUCKINGHAMSHIRE: Anthony Mackay. Superb line drawings plus background text: large format landscape gift book.

BUCKINGHAMSHIRE MURDERS: Len Woodley. Nearly two centuries of nasty crimes.

WINGRAVE: A Rothschild Village in the Vale: Margaret and Ken Morley. Thoroughly researched and copiously illustrated survey of the last 200 years in this lovely village between Aylesbury and Leighton Buzzard.

HISTORIC FIGURES IN THE BUCKINGHAMSHIRE LANDSCAPE: John Houghton. Major personalities and events that have shaped the county's past, including Bletchley Park.

TWICE UPON A TIME: John Houghton. North Bucks short stories loosely based on fact.

SANCTITY AND SCANDAL IN BEDS AND BUCKS: John Houghton. A miscellany of unholy people and events.

MANORS and MAYHEM, PAUPERS and PARSONS: Tales from Four Shires: Beds., Bucks., Herts. and Northants: John Houghton. Little known historical snippets and stories.

FOLK: Characters and Events in the History of Bedfordshire and Northamptonshire: Vivienne Evans. Anthology of people of yesteryear - arranged alphabetically by village or town.

JOHN BUNYAN: His Life and Times: Vivienne Evans. Highly praised and readable account.

THE RAILWAY AGE IN BEDFORDSHIRE: Fred Cockman. Classic, illustrated account of early railway history.

A LASTING IMPRESSION: Michael Dundrow. A boyhood evacuee recalls his years in the Chiltern village of Totternhoe near Dunstable.

GLEANINGS REVISITED: Nostalgic Thoughts of a Bedfordshire Farmer's Boy: E.W. O'Dell. His own sketches and early photographs adorn this lively account of rural Bedfordshire in days gone by.

BEDFORDSHIRE'S YESTERYEARS Vol 2: The Rural Scene: Brenda Fraser-Newstead. Vivid first-hand accounts of country life two or three generations ago.

BEDFORDSHIRE'S YESTERYEARS Vol 3: Craftsmen and Tradespeople: Brenda Fraser-Newstead. Fascinating recollections over several generations practising many vanishing crafts and trades.

BEDFORDSHIRE'S YESTERYEARS Vol 4: War Times and Civil Matters: Brenda Fraser-Newstead. Two World Wars, plus transport, law and order, etc.

PROUD HERITAGE: A Brief History of Dunstable, 1000-2000AD: Vivienne Evans. Century by century account of the town's rich tradition and key events, many of national significance.

DUNSTABLE WITH THE PRIORY: 1100-1550: Vivienne Evans. Dramatic growth of Henry I's important new town around a major crossroads.

DUNSTABLE IN TRANSITION: 1550-1700: Vivienne Evans. Wealth of original material as the town evolves without the Priory.

DUNSTABLE DECADE: THE EIGHTIES: A Collection of Photographs: Pat Lovering. A souvenir book of nearly 300 pictures of people and events in the 1980s.

STREETS AHEAD: An Illustrated Guide to the Origins of Dunstable's Street Names: Richard Walden. Fascinating text and captions to hundreds of photographs, past and present, throughout the town.

DUNSTABLE IN DETAIL: Nigel Benson. A hundred of the town's buildings and features, plus town trail map.

OLD DUNSTABLE: Bill Twaddle. A new edition of this collection of early photographs.

BOURNE and BRED: A Dunstable Boyhood Between the Wars: Colin Bourne. An elegantly written, well illustrated book capturing the spirit of the town over fifty years ago.

OLD HOUGHTON: Pat Lovering. Pictorial record capturing the changing appearances of Houghton Regis over the past 100 years.

ROYAL HOUGHTON: Pat Lovering. Illustrated history of Houghton Regis from the earliest of times to the present.

THE STOPSLEY BOOK: James Dyer. Definitive, detailed account of this historic area of Luton. 150 rare photographs.

THE STOPSLEY PICTURE BOOK: James Dyer. New material and photographs make an ideal companion to The Stopsley Book.

PUBS and PINTS: The Story of Luton's Public Houses and Breweries: Stuart Smith. The background to beer in the town, plus hundreds of photographs, old and new.

LUTON AT WAR I: As compiled by the Luton News in 1947, a well illustrated thematic account.

THE CHANGING FACE OF LUTON: An Illustrated History: Stephen Bunker, Robin Holgate and Marian Nichols. Luton's development from earliest times to the present busy industrial town. Illustrated in colour and mono.

WHERE THEY BURNT THE TOWN HALL DOWN: Luton, The First World War and the Peace Day Riots, July 1919: Dave Craddock. Detailed analysis of a notorious incident.

THE MEN WHO WORE STRAW HELMETS: Policing Luton, 1840-1974: Tom Madigan. Fine chronicled history, many rare photographs; author~served in Luton Police for fifty years.

BETWEEN THE HILLS: The Story of Lilley, a Chiltern Village: Roy Pinnock. A priceless piece of our heritage - the rural beauty remains but the customs and way of life described here have largely disappeared.

KENILWORTH SUNSET: A Luton Town Supporter's Journal: Tim Kingston. Frank and funny account of football's ups and downs.

A HATTER GOES MAD!: Kristina Howells. Luton Town footballers, officials and supporters talk to a female fan.

LEGACIES: Tales and Legends of Luton and the North Chilterns: Vic Lea. Mysteries and stories based on fact, including Luton Town Football Club. Many photographs.

THREADS OF TIME: Shela Porter. The life of a remarkable mother and businesswoman, spanning the entire century and based in Hitchin and (mainly) Bedford.

LEAFING THROUGH LITERATURE: Writers' Lives in Herts and Beds: David Carroll. Illustrated short biographies of many famous authors and their connections with these counties.

A PILGRIMAGE IN HERTFORDSHIRE: H.M. Alderman. Classic, between-the-wars tour round the county, embellished with line drawings.

THE VALE OF THE NIGHTINGALE: Molly Andrews. Several generations of a family, lived against a Harpenden backdrop.

SUGAR MICE AND STICKLEBACKS: Childhood Memories of a Hertfordshire Lad: Harry Edwards.Vivid evocation of gentle pre-war in an archetypal village, Hertingfordbury.

SWANS IN MY KITCHEN: Lis Dorer. Story of a Swan Sanctuary near Hemel Hempstead.

THE HILL OF THE MARTYR: An Architectural History of St.Albans Abbey: Eileen Roberts. Scholarly and readable chronological narrative history of Hertfordshire and Bedfordshire's famous cathedral. Fully illustrated with photographs and plans.

CHILTERN ARCHAEOLOGY: RECENT WORK: A Handbook for the Next Decade: edited by Robin Holgate. The latest views, results and excavations by twenty-three leading archaeologists throughout the Chilterns.

THE TALL HITCHIN INSPECTOR'S CASEBOOK: A Victorian Crime Novel Based on Fact: Edgar Newman. Worthies of the time encounter more archetypal villains.

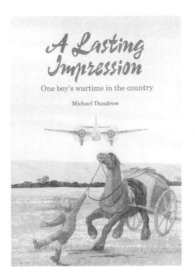

A LASTING IMPRESSION
by Michael Dundrow

Michael Dundrow experienced an event in his formative years, which strongly coloured or even completely changed the rest of his life.

This book describes one boy's overwhelming experience - wartime evacuation which has left a truly lasting impression on his adult life. For this twelve year old from London's East End, to be dumped among a family of strangers on a large and busy farm below the Chilterns in Bedfordshire was a make or break experience of the first order.

Enriched by his years on the farm and in the village of Totternhoe, the adventures with new found friends, the sheer interest, fun and hard work of farm life and also the sowing of the seeds of appreciation of that lovely corner of South Bedfordshire, the details are all here, written with great affection. Although written fifty years after these unforgettable things happened, the story is undimmed by the passage of time.

In this evocative picture of wartime England are many glimpses of a way of village and farm life that has altered so dramatically in recent years as to be almost unrecognisable today.

A Book Castle Publication

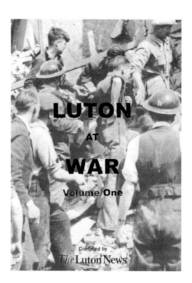

LUTON AT WAR

Initially published by the Luton News in 1947, the story of how the people of Luton withstood the dark years of war between 1939 and 1945. Luton and its population have changed so dramatically in the years since the war that now only a few will recall how the town stood up to the trauma of those war years.

Because of strict war-time censorship much of what occurred during those years was not mentioned in The Luton News. Once the war was over however, The Luton News set about the mammoth task of presenting a complete and vivid picture of war-time life. It tells of the long anxious nights, the joy and the sorrow that made even the most terrifying moments bearable thanks to the tremendous way in which the people joined to help each other.

Written and compiled by the staff of The Luton News at the time, it contains the most comprehensive and fascinating pictorial record. As well as being a moving personal account it is also a unique historical document. Published in a large format paperback in two parts - volume 1 in autumn 2000 and volume 2 in autumn 2001.

A Book Castle Publication

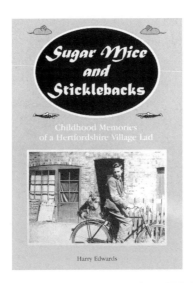

SUGAR MICE AND STICKLEBACKS
by Harry Edwards

Memories of a typical English village, Hertingfordbury, in the pre-war days when life was slower and gentler...

When the grocer, baker, cobbler, tailor, post-office, sweet-shop and builder's yard were all close at hand; the milk was delivered in a horse drawn cart. Facilities included a village school, a branch-line railway station, a Memorial Hall, a cricket pitch and pavilion, and the imposing Church of St. Mary with its Old Rectory. A vivid picture of country life is conjured up.

Harry Edwards was born in a cottage next to the mill, and enjoyed a close family life. The luxuries of his mother's home-made cakes and pastries, his father's home grown produce, the early impact of radio and eventually main sewerage!

A sequel 'Sticks and Stones' covering Harry's career as a Journeyman Printer in Hertford, Dunstable, Cheltenham and Wolverton is published in 2001.

Boyhood pleasures only needed a simple stick or ball; hours of fun could be found just sorting out mother's button tin; or a more ambitious project could lead to a rickety trolley or punt. A special joy to Harry as a youngster was splashing about with the gang in the endlessly fascinating river - or fishing by jar for sticklebacks in the extensive watercress beds.

A Book Castle Publication